The Hindu Vatican

Suresh Chandra Agarwal

PARTRIDGE

To order additional copies of this book, contact
Partridge India
000 800 10062 62
orders.india@partridgepublishing.com

www.partridgepublishing.com/india

Dedicated To

My late elder brothers,
Shri Satishchandra Agarwal
and
Shri Naveenchandra Agarwal

Contents

Preface

The Hindus take pride in the fact that their religion is the oldest on earth, surviving since about five thousand years without an apex governing body or an apex priest.

There is no doubt that Hinduism can still survive for thousands of years more without having an apex governing body as well as an apex priest, but certain developments during the last two to three decades in India, in my opinion, have necessitated the need of an apex governing body of Hinduism as well as an apex priest to head it.

Seventy years have gone by after India got its independence from the British. The scheduled castes and scheduled tribes were given certain benefits in the Constitution of India in the form of reservation in political constituencies and government jobs as well as admission into government schools and colleges. The framers of the Constitution of India did so to provide a level playing field to the scheduled castes and scheduled tribes as they had suffered from their social and economic backwardness for centuries. But the framers of the constitution did not intend to provide such reservation benefits endlessly.

Not only does the reservation system for the scheduled castes and scheduled tribes continue to this day but the political parties have also added many backward classes to the list of beneficiaries for the reservation system. The situation has reached such a point that no political party can dare to speak of the withdrawal of the reservation benefits for any caste. One who does so is likely to be out of politics.

In my opinion, the only valid option available for Hinduism is to abolish the entire caste system from it. That is the only solution to get rid of the negative competition among political parties to win over different castes and communities. The political parties cannot be relied on to have a consensus on this matter as any political party initiating the move is likely to go out of politics at the earliest, but if there is an apex governing body of Hinduism and it abolishes the entire caste system, the political parties can hold that body responsible for doing so and escape any criticism.

The formation of an apex governing body of Hinduism is the only answer.

Since 2014, the Bharatiya Janata Party, the right wing Hindu party, has been in power at the centre and also ruled in many states. It has vigorously taken the issue of cow protection, and with no apex Hindu body to look after the task, the government itself is carrying out the task of cow protection. Many states governed by the BJP have separate ministries related to cow protection. There have been incidences involving overenthusiastic cow protectors as well as some antisocial elements working under the disguise of cow protection. The ruling governments are held responsible for such incidences.

The Bharatiya Janata Party has championed the cause of Hinduism in India, and the formation of an apex governing body during its tenure is only going to add a feather in its cap. Such formation will also help the ruling party to concentrate more on governance. Along with cow protection, the country also needs a better education system, better healthcare system, better judiciary, better care for elders, and positive action on many other issues. The creation of an apex governing body in Hinduism is going to help the government immensely as it will be able to concentrate more on other issues and leave all religious matters to the apex governing body.

I have given the name Maha Mandir to the proposed apex governing body of Hinduism. I hope the readers will find the book interesting.

Suresh Agarwal
January 2018
Ahmedabad, India

The Idea of a Hindu Vatican

One of my morning-walk friends, Mr Mehta, arrived back at his home after a guided tour of Europe last summer. Since then, even after a few months had passed, but he was still suffering from the hangover of his European trip. In the morning, when we walked along with him, he was not tired of narrating his experience of European tour. He would go on to the extent that some friends started to feel bored while some feel jealous.

The dictionary meaning of the word *hangover* is a headache one goes through after an excessive intake of alcohol. In India a person can have a sort of hangover in many ways. If a person is highly impressed by a speech of a saint or a spiritual guru or by a speaker in a seminar, he goes on talking about it for weeks to his friends and relatives. He narrates it as if he had a heavenly experience. Similarly, if one guy whose son's marriage has taken place recently and all the marriage functions have been well attended and praised by the guests too, the guy may suffer from hangover of success of the marriage functions for a long time. It will only be over when his daughter-in-law gets pregnant.

1

Another form of hangover comes from the successful house-warming of somebody's new house. In India the people build houses for two purposes. One is obviously to have somewhere they can reside in comfortably, and second is to show their relatives, friends, and society that now they have become rich or richer than before. Sometimes this hangover also lasts till all the bills related to its construction as well as the interior are paid.

There are hangovers of other kinds also, but I had a good idea of what Mr Mehta's hangover was. Once, he was boasting about his visit to Vatican. 'See, neither do you have to take off your shoes nor switch off your mobile. You are also not restrained from taking photographs with a mobile or a camera.' He goes on further, 'And what cleanliness and silence!'

In the Vatican, there are no restrictions on people from any other faith or religion. Above all, the Vatican enjoys the status of being the smallest country on earth. Why does our Hinduism not have a Vatican sort of place or a Hindu pope to head the Hindu religion?

It looked as if my other morning-walk friends were not interested. It was maybe because Mr Mehta lectured us daily about his European tour and my other friends might have not listened to him carefully.

But yes, I got the idea. Why do we Hindus not have a Vatican of our own and an apex religious priest to head it?

I searched Google and was amazed to learn that Vatican has less than one square kilometre area. In India our highly respected yogis and gurus have ashrams spread over well beyond the area the Vatican has. Many of our temples have tons of gold worth billions of dollars, lying in their treasure vaults or in the banks. I have visited the Akshardham temple at Delhi and also at Gandhinagar, Gujarat. I have also heard of many

Swaminarayan temples built abroad in the UK, USA, and other countries.

So I am quite convinced that the place for a Hindu Vatican, if we go for it, is not going to be a problem. We have enough resources in the form of gold lying within a number of temples and our Swaminarayan temple devotees also have necessary expertise to build the Hindu Vatican in a short period.

So why not to go for it?

The Hindu religion is the oldest religion on earth, much older than Christianity, Islam, Buddhism, Jainism, Sikhism, or any other surviving religion. The Hindu religion has survived for thousands of years without an apex priest and a sort of Vatican to accommodate him. It can also continue to survive for thousands of coming years in the future without an apex priest or a governing body. I personally feel that after seventy years of independence from the British, a Hindu Vatican is the need of the hour.

The caste system is an evil giving bad name to Hindus the world over. Only an apex body of Hinduism can dare to get rid of the caste system prevailing in Hindu society. Dr Ambedkar, the champion of the cause of Dalits and chief architect of the constitution of India did recommend the reservation of seats for Dalits as a tool for a level playing field in politics, government jobs, and education imparted by the government. But during the last seventy years after the independence, the politicians have not only added the backward classes but are also supporting the other left-behind castes (other than the Dalits and scheduled castes) to join the bandwagon. The situation has reached a point of no return. Any political party who dares to reverse the reservation system is likely to get kicked out of politics.

Now it is only a sort of Hindu Vatican, the seat of an apex Hindu priest, which can save the country from the caste system. The caste system has been a severe blot on Hindu society for thousands of years. It has spread to other religions as well in and around India. The Muslims in Pakistan and the Buddhist in Sri Lanka do have a caste system functioning in one or other form. The Sikh religion, which is the most junior of all the religions, also has its 25 per cent population in a lower caste category. Strangely, the Hindus and the Sikhs who have moved to other parts of the world continue to follow casteism in a manner that the natives of those countries rate the Indians as the most racist people on earth.

The Bharatiya Janata Party under the leadership of Mr Modi has restored the pride among the Indian Hindus domestically, the Hindus in foreign soil are disregarded for the caste system they have in their religion. It is time to bid goodbye to the evil of casteism, and only a sort of Hindu Vatican can do so.

The BJP, the ruling party at the centre as well as many states in India, has also unleashed the wave of cow protection, which is the core belief of Hindus all over the world. Even Mahatma Gandhi supported cow protection, and the Constitution of India is also against cow slaughtering in spite of India being a secular country. There are thousands of cows roaming free on Indian roads in urban as well as rural areas, causing injuries to citizens at times. There are also roaming cows eating away the crops in fields, causing disharmony among farmers and dairy farmers. In spite of strict laws on cow protection in a number of states, lakhs of cows reach slaughterhouses, and cows in even bigger numbers are smuggled to Bangladesh by an established network.

The new apex Hindu body can fully take on cow protection. It will leave more time for the Indian government to concentrate on other issues of governance.

The Evil of the Caste System in India

The main motivation behind the creation of this book, *The Hindu Vatican*, by me is to put some efforts in the direction of eradicating the evil of the caste system in India.

The Indians have been blaming the Britishers for their divide and rule policy and for the many evils in Indian society. I find by reading the history of India during the period of colonial rule of the British that historians have blamed the British for encouraging the caste system in India. The historians say that the British showed discrimination towards certain castes while recruiting persons for government jobs. I don't take it as fully correct.

For centuries, the caste system has been practised in India, and it is among the world's oldest forms of surviving social stratification. The system which divides Hindus into rigid hierarchical groups based on their karma (work) and dharma (the Hindu word for *religion*, but here it means *duty*) is generally accepted to be more than three thousand years old.

Manu-smriti, widely regarded to be the most important and authoritative book on Hindu law and dating back to at least a thousand years before Christ was born, 'acknowledges and justifies the caste system as the basis of order and regularity of society'.

The caste system divides Hindus into four main categories: Brahmans, Kshatriyas, Vaisyas, and Shudras. Many believe that the groups originated from Brahma, the Hindu god of creation.

At the top of the hierarchy are the Brahmans, who were mainly teachers and intellectuals and are believed to have come from Brahma's head. Then come the Kshatriyas, or the warrior and rulers, supposedly from his arms. The third slot is to the Vaisyas, or the traders, who were created from his thighs. At the bottom of the heap are the Shudras, who came from Brahma's feet and do all the menial jobs.

The main castes are further divided into about three thousand castes and twenty-five thousand subcastes, each based on their specific occupation.

Outside of this Hindu caste system are the Dalits—the *achhoots* or the untouchables.

For centuries, caste dictated almost every aspect of Hindu religious and social life, with each group occupying a specific place in this complex hierarchy.

Rural communities were long arranged on the basis of castes. The upper and lower castes almost always lived in segregated colonies. The water wells were not shared. Brahmans would not accept food or drink from the Shudras. And one could marry only within one's caste.

Traditionally, the system bestowed many privileges on the upper castes while sanctioned repression of the lower castes by privileged groups. Despite all the obstacles, however, some Dalits and other low-caste Indians, such as B. R. Ambedkar (who authored the

Constitution of India) and K. R. Narayanan (who became the nation's president), have risen to hold prestigious positions in the country. The present president of India, Ram Nath Kovind, also hails from the Dalit community.

Independent constitution banned discrimination on the basis of caste, and in an attempt to correct historical injustice and provide a level playing field to the traditionally disadvantaged, the authorities announced quotas in government jobs and educational institutions for scheduled castes and scheduled tribes, the lowest in the caste hierarchy, in 1950.

In 1989, quotas were extended to include a grouping called the OBC (other backward classes), which fall between the traditional upper castes and lowest.

In recent decades, with the spread of secular education and growing urbanization, the influence of caste has somewhat declined, especially in cities where different castes live side by side and intercaste marriage are becoming more common.

In certain southern states and in the northern states of Bihar, many people have begun using just one name after social reform movements. Despite the changes, though, caste identities remain strong, and last names are almost always indications of what caste a person belongs to.

In recent years, there have been demands from several communities to be recognized as OBCs. Last year, at least eighteen people have been killed in violent protests by the Jat community in Haryana. The Patel community led huge protests in Gujarat, demanding access to caste quotas. The Marathas in Maharashtra have staged a huge demonstration to include their community in OBCs this year. All these communities are prosperous and politically dominant communities, but they support their demand for caste quotas by saying large numbers in their communities are poor and suffering.

Recently, some politicians and Dalit leaders have emphasized the need for job reservation in the private sector. There has been a gathering at Ramlila Maidan in Delhi to press the demand for the same. The leaders insist that there has been very little creation of jobs for the Dalits in government departments in few decades and that many people have been employed on a contract basis, which does not attract the reservation.

Even seventy years after independence, Dalits and Adivasis continue to face mind-boggling social discrimination and spine-chilling atrocities across the country. One in four Indians admits to practising caste untouchability in some form in their homes. This shocking fact has been revealed by a mega pan-India survey conducted by the National Council of Applied Economic Research (NCAER) and University of Maryland, USA. Indians belonging to virtually every religious and caste group—including Muslims, Christians, scheduled castes, and scheduled tribes— admit to practising untouchability, shows the India Human Development Survey (IDHS-II) of 2011–12. Mere tokenism and lip service will not do. India needs to jettison the centuries-old dehumanizing baggage of caste stigma once and for all. It should have nothing to hide, and we should see the reality as it is and confront the issues involved head on towards a transformation.

If India has to move ahead to a caste-free nation, the need is for Indian to have an all-embracing, all-inclusive movement for social and cultural transformation. Ambedkar showed the way: 'Turn in any direction you like. Caste is the evil that crosses your path. You cannot have political reforms. You cannot have economic reform unless you kill this evil.'

The caste system in Hinduism has influenced other religions like Buddhism, Christianity, Islam, and Sikhism in Southeast Asia.

Although the Sikh gurus criticized the hierarchy of the caste system, one does exist in the Sikh community. According to Surinder S. Jodhka, the Sikh religion does not advocate discrimination against any caste or creed; however, in practice, Sikhs belonging to the dominant landowning castes have not shed all their prejudices against the Dalits. While Dalits would be allowed entry into the village gurdwaras, they would not be permitted to cook or serve langar (the communal meal). Therefore, wherever they could mobilize resources, the Dalits of Punjab have tried to construct their own gurdwara and other local-level institutions in order to attain a certain degree of cultural autonomy.

Talking about the distribution of Indian population by religion and caste categories, Hinduism in India has 26 per cent population of forward-caste communities, about 43 per cent population of backward-caste communities, 22 per cent population of scheduled caste communities, and 9 per cent population of scheduled tribes communities.

Islam in India has about 60 per cent population of forward-caste communities, about 39 per cent population of backward-class communities, and only about 1 per cent population of scheduled caste and scheduled tribes communities.

The Christians in India have about 33 per cent population of forward-caste communities, about 25 per cent population of backward-class communities, about 33 per cent population of scheduled tribe communities, and 9 per cent population of scheduled castes communities.

The Sikhs in India have about 46 per cent population of forward-caste communities, about 23 per cent population of backward-class communities, about

31 per cent population of scheduled caste communities. The part of scheduled tribe communities in Sikhism is very negligible.

Interestingly, almost the entire population of Buddhists in India are of scheduled caste communities and scheduled tribes communities.

There has been criticism of the Hindu caste system both within and outside India. Since 1980 it has become a major issue in politics of India.

The caste system has been criticized by many Hindu reformers in the past. Jyotirao Phule (1827–1890) vehemently criticized any explanations that the caste system was natural and ordained by the Creator in Hindu texts. If Brahma wanted castes, argued Phule, he would have ordained the same for other creatures. There are no castes in species of animals or birds, so why should there be one among human animals? In his criticism, Phule added, 'Brahmans cannot claim superior status because of caste, because they hardly bothered with these when wining and dining with Europeans.' Professions do not make castes, and castes do not decide one's profession. If someone does a job that is dirty, it does not make them inferior; in the same way, no mother is inferior because she cleans the excreta of her baby. Ritual occupation or tasks, argued Phule, do not make any human being superior or inferior.

Swami Vivekananda similarly criticized caste system as one of the many human institutions that bars the power of free thought and action of an individual. Caste or no caste, creed or no creed, any man or class or caste or nation or institution that bars the power of free thought and bars action of an individual is devilish and must go down. Liberty of thought and action, asserted Vivekananda, is the only condition of life, of growth, and of well-being.

Dr Bhimrao Ambedkar was born in a caste that was classified as untouchable. He became a leader of human rights in India, a prolific writer, and a key person in drafting modern India's constitution in the 1940s. He wrote extensively on discrimination, trauma, and what he saw as the tragic effects of the caste system in India.

Mahatma Gandhi—in his younger years, Gandhi—disagreed with some of Ambedkar's observations, rationale, and interpretations about the caste system in India. 'Caste', he claimed, 'has saved Hinduism from disintegration. But like every other institution, it has suffered from excrescences.' He considered the four divisions of varnas to be fundamental, natural, and essential. The innumerable subcastes or jatis he considered to be a hindrance. He advocated to fuse all the jatis into a more global division of varnas. In the 1930s, Gandhi began to advocate for the idea of heredity in caste to be rejected, arguing, 'Assumption of superiority by any person over any other is a sin against God and man. Thus caste system, in so far as it connotes distinctions in status, is an evil.'

He claimed that *varnashrama* of the shashtras is today non-existent in practice. The present caste system is the theory antithesis of varnashrama. Caste in its current form, claimed Gandhi, had nothing to do with religion. The discrimination and trauma of castes, argued Gandhi, was the result of custom, the origin of which is unknown. Gandhi said that the customs' origin was a moot point because one could spiritually sense that customs were wrong and that any caste system is harmful to the spiritual well-being of man and the economic well-being of a nation. The reality of colonial India was that, Gandhi noted, there was no significant disparity between the economic condition and earnings of members of different castes, whether it was a Brahman or an artisan or a farmer of low caste. India was poor, and Indians of all castes were poor. Thus, he argued that the cause of trauma was not in the caste system but elsewhere. Judged by the standards being applied to India, Gandhi said, every human society would fail. Gandhi believed that one must consider the best if produced as well, along with the vast majority in impoverished Indian villages struggling to make ends meet, with woes of which there was little knowledge.

Mahatma Gandhi did take the support of Dalits during his struggle for the freedom of India and gave them a name, Harijan, but it seems that he was little confused about the caste system in Hinduism, he himself being from the superior caste Vaisya.

After the independence of India, no Hindu activists or reformist has dared to criticize the caste system in Hinduism. The congress party ruled India single-handedly for almost three decades and treated the Dalits as a vote bank. Thereafter, other political parties also went on to compete in congress to create separate vote banks for them and brought backward classes into their vote bank. Any political spokesman who spoke against the caste system after the independence of India either had to take back his words or step down from his position.

Seventy years have gone by since India gained its independence from the British. Every Hindu knows well that the caste system is an evil in Hinduism and it has to be eradicated. We cannot rely on political parties or the social activists to do so. Perhaps a Hindu apex authority can do so.

The Caste System in Hinduism: A Challenge for the Maha Mandir

The Hindu Vatican, or by whatever name we call it, could be Maha Mandir. We may address the apex priest of Hinduism as Maha Mahant Sree. We may also address the apex governing body of Maha Mandir as Shikhar Samiti and a member of apex body as Shikhar Samiti Sabhya.

There are so many tasks the Maha Mandir can perform or take up. The first and foremost task is to abolish the prevailing caste system in the Hindu religion. As we go through the old texts on Hindu religion, we will see that few people consider the caste system as an evil in Hindu society. There are so many who try to justify that the caste system in Hinduism has been flexible and one could switch over to a higher caste by virtue of one's karma. Such people do not see the caste system as a curse on the Hindu society.

Billions of Hindus might have been born during the years (about five thousand) of the existence of Hinduism. Just imagine the plight of Hindus born as Dalits during these five thousand years and the hatred, agony they faced in day-to-day life.

They were treated inhumanely or as lesser humans in comparison to the people of other castes. They were forced to stay in separate settlements at a distance from a village or a town. The homes they lived in were dirty and filthy. People from the higher castes even treated the shadow of a Dalit as a bad omen. In many villages, the Dalits were forced to walk with a hanging broom tied to their back, which would clean the path they walked on. A bulk of them carried human waste on their heads for centuries. Even during the early years post the independence, during pre-Holi festival days, some notorious elements would force a Dalit to carry a pot filled with human waste on his head, and then they'd break the pot by throwing a stone at it. It happened more in the northern part of India. Can one imagine the scenario of putting his or her child through this kind of inhumane behaviour?

Mahatma Gandhi did a good job by accepting the Dalits into the fold of India's freedom struggle. He gave the name Harijan to the Dalits. There is no evidence in history that Mahatma Gandhi even thought of removing the entire caste system from Hinduism. Still, he can be given the benefit of the doubt because his main task was to get freedom for India from the British. Had he fought for the abolishment of the caste system simultaneously with the freedom fight, he would have lost the support of higher-caste Hindus, which the British would have liked.

The Hindu Dalits had a true champion fighting for their cause in Dr Bhimrao Ambedkar. But he himself being a Dalit could have a limited appeal on higher-caste Hindus had he gone to fight for the total abolishment of the caste system. The history of the entire world reveals that always there has been an oppressor who understood the problem of the oppressed class and then used it in their favour. A leader of the oppressed class has definitely helped in their struggle, but ultimately, the leader from the section of oppressors won the battle for them. The slavery system was abolished by Abraham Lincoln and not by a slave. The list is endless. Dr Ambedkar could not have done it, so he only asked for the benefits of his fellow Dalits. The caste system can only be removed from the Hindu religion by a leader from the so-called higher Hindu caste or a religious high priest.

It has been more than seventy years since India won its independence from the British. The scheduled castes and the scheduled tribes were given some level playing field in the form of reserved seats in parliament and state assemblies. They were also given reservations in central government jobs as well as state government jobs in addition to reservations in government schools and colleges. The SC and ST families who reaped the benefits of the reservation policy in the 1950s are now into their third generation but are still reaping the benefits of the reservation system. In fact, since they know the game better and have the right contacts, the ordinary people from SC and ST families have fewer chances in getting into government jobs and government educational institutes. There has been talk of the 'creamy layer' sometime back, but the powerful lobby of SC/ST officers somehow manages to see that they are not deprived of reservation benefits.

The reservation for other backward classes is a new phenomenon that has existed for a little over three decades now. It has created a sort of negative competition among all the so-called other backward classes, and every caste and community is now working hard to jump on to the bandwagon. During the last few years, the agitations of the Patidars in Gujarat, the Jats in Haryana, the Gurjars in Rajasthan, and recently, the Marathas in Maharashtra have resulted in heavy loss of government property and lives in addition to loss of millions of man-hours. There does not seem to be any end to such agitations in the near future. Maybe some new communities will start agitations in some other states to join the list of other backward classes; only time will say. The political parties simply are helpless in this matter.

The young generations from so-called higher Hindu castes have their own questions. They don't understand the rationale behind the loss of opportunities for them in job reservations as well as quotas in government educational institutions against the Dalits and other backward classes.

The people from SC and ST families who got government jobs during the last seventy years still do not command the necessary respect from other castes. The people from higher Hindu castes and communities are not comfortable in mixing with them. There are separate messes for SC/ST in the police department as well as in the paramilitary forces. Dr Ambedkar wanted his fellow community members to be treated at par with other Hindu castes, which does not seem to be possible even in the distant future. The people from SC/ST families still suffer from very low-esteem with no end to it. The Indians in overseas countries also continue the practice of hatred towards SC/ST families. The higher-caste Indians don't mix with the SC/ST Indians who have migrated abroad for jobs. How long are the people from scheduled castes and scheduled tribes going to suffer a life of undignified humans in the eyes of so-called higher-caste Hindus?

The caste system in Hinduism is in the DNA of every Hindu. Sometimes, even a Dalit is proud of being from a Dalit caste that is a little superior to a fellow Dalit. There are no marriage relations possible between two such Dalit castes. All the major castes—whether Shudra, Vaisya, Brahman, or Kshatriya—have hundreds of subcastes. Each subcaste claims to be superior than the other subcastes, and it is difficult for arranged marriages between the two subcastes.

The Hindu religion, the oldest in existence on earth since about five thousand years, has been without an apex governing body and apex religious priest. Many invaders from foreign soils have come and gone but have succeeded in getting converted very few Hindus to other religions. In spite of all the hardships and indignity faced by Dalits, very few of them have taken up other religions. This fact encourages the ordinary Hindus to take pride in the fact that there is something great that make Hindus stand tall against all the odds and that too without any apex body or an apex priest.

The Bharatiya Janata Party, since it came to power at the centre in 2014, has restored the pride of Hindus before the Muslims as well as other minorities but not before all the religions throughout the world. It is an unwritten practice all over the world that people shouldn't fault others, so people from other religions outside India don't say to the face of Hindus, 'Your caste system is not fair.' But Hindus are considered as racist people on earth. The general impression is that for a Hindu, the caste, the language, and the colour of one's skin, along with one's religion, come first before treating anyone as a human being.

Many advanced countries have peaked up economically, and China too is going to join them in ten to twenty years. It is India's turn now. At present, being more than 17 per cent of the world population, India enjoys less than 3 per cent of the world's GDP. India has enormous scope to move up the economic ladder with least efforts. Before India completes 100 years of its independence, it will be definitely treated as a middle-income nation. By the year 2047, the Indian population may touch the figure of 20 per cent of world population, and its GDP may grow from the present 3 per cent to 7–8 per cent of the world's GDP. No other nation in the world has such a chance.

Do we want to be seen as the most racist people on earth even in year 2047? How will the souls of Mahatma Gandhi and Dr Ambedkar feel then? Seventy years have passed by, and thirty more years may not take much time. We cannot rely on our political parties to take the caste system out of Hinduism. It has been prevalent for thousands of years. The only remedy which comes to my mind is that it is high time that we have an apex governing body in Hinduism along with an apex priest.

There are more than a billion Hindus in India today along with tens of millions in other countries around the world. Only the Christians and the Muslims are more in number than the Hindus. The Vatican, the seat of the pope, enjoys the status of being the smallest nation on earth, with only an area of about 0.7 square kilometres. The pope is a binding factor for all Catholic Christians on earth. The Vatican frequently issues advisories to all the fellow Christians. For many centuries, the pope has been successful in creating values in the lives of all fellow Christians.

Casteism in Hinduism is now fast developing into a monstrous proposition. Before the British left and before the rise of Dr Ambedkar, all the backward-class Hindus, Dalits, and the scheduled tribes took their social and financial positions as fate decided by their god. Dr Ambedkar is responsible for creating awareness among Dalits and the scheduled tribe that they deserve treatment at par with other Hindus. Dr Ambedkar demanded political reservation only as a level playing field since the people from scheduled caste and scheduled tribes needed some space before they could attain equality with the rest of the Hindus. He did not think that the reservation system could go on endlessly.

The benefits this would bring to the backward classes other than scheduled castes and scheduled tribes have been used as a ploy by some political parties to eat into the vote bank of the congress party, which has ruled India since 1947. Now with the ongoing agitations in Rajasthan, Gujarat, Haryana, and Maharashtra by the Jats, Patidars, Gurjars, and Marathas, it is imperative that the Hindus look for an umbrella in the form of an apex body to govern all the matters related to Hinduism.

Before the Maha Mandir is able to abolish the caste system in Hinduism, it is also imperative that the government comes out with a direct fund transfer scheme in bank accounts for the very poor, the poor, and the lower middle income sections of the society. Almost 60 per cent of the population of India belongs to these sections. If the caste system is abolished and the present system of subsidies continues, there is bound to be chaos. The poor and underprivileged people of India (which is half its population and belongs to scheduled castes, scheduled tribes, and many backward castes) depend on the present subsidized prices of certain items for consumption along with an illusionary hope of getting government jobs and getting into government colleges and schools. Once the 'direct fund transfer to one's bank account' scheme is in place, all the people of poor and underprivileged sections irrespective of their castes and communities are going to have some additional purchasing power in their hands.

Only one out of twenty—say 5 per cent of people belonging to scheduled castes, scheduled tribes, and some backward castes succeed in getting a job in central government, state government, local civic bodies, or any government institutions. The 'direct fund transfer into bank accounts' scheme is going to benefit the rest— ninety-five per cent of the people in the form of additional cash or purchasing power in their hands.

If the present system continues, one out of twenty people may get a government job, but the rest (nineteen people) have to spend their lives buying many things for consumption—like grains, pulses, kerosene, gas, sugar, and so many other items—at subsidized prices. Still, many people from these poor and underprivileged sections have very little purchasing power to buy things even at subsidized prices. The direct transfer of funds into their bank account is going to give them some purchasing power, which is going to be at least Rs.1,500 per month for each family. The cash transfer scheme is going to be for all the poor and underprivileged sections of society, irrespective of their castes. This fact itself is going to bring all the Hindus at par with each other.

At present, the poor families from the castes belonging to the so-called higher strata do not get any benefits of reservation in government jobs or admissions in government schools and colleges compared to the established backward classes. Often, the government says that the quota includes the poorest section of higher-caste Hindus, but practically, it does not seem possible. A 'direct fund transfer to bank accounts' scheme along with the total abolition of the caste system in Hinduism is going to satisfy all.

Still there are going to be some political parties along with their leaders claiming to be the champions of scheduled castes, scheduled tribes, and some backward classes that show dislike towards the abolition of the caste system because they will not be able to sell any illusionary dreams to the voters in the form of the reservation system.

Many Hindus may not like the idea of abolishing the caste system from Hinduism since the people, particularly those from the so-called higher Hindu castes, take pride in being a Brahman, Vaisya, or Kshatriya. These people are not comfortable at all in sitting along with the so-called lower-caste people. The notions developed in these so-called higher-caste people are thousands of years old and cannot be expected to go overnight. Still I am quite sure that these higher-caste people will not be able to oppose the abolition of the caste system. The caste system in Hinduism has no justification or rationale in modern civil societies; neither is there anything parallel to it in other religions throughout the world. If the Muslims and Buddhists in Sri Lanka, Pakistan, Nepal, or Bangladesh have some sort of caste system, it is because of the influence of Hinduism over a period of hundreds of years. The abolition of the caste system from Hinduism is going to benefit all the religions in neighbouring countries.

The abolition of the caste system may bring certain new problems. Who is going to undertake the jobs related to civic sanitation? At present, the Dalits and scheduled tribes are doing all these jobs, and sometimes the government pays them well. Once the caste system is abolished, there is going to be competition from all other castes to get into better jobs. Seventy years is not a small period for the scheduled castes and scheduled tribes to get better education and get into jobs other than sanitation. Once the caste system is abolished, the people from the present scheduled castes will have more opportunities to get better jobs as well as better education for their children. It will only benefit them in the long run. The biggest benefit is that their self-esteem shall be restored.

At present, particularly in rural areas, the Dalits are not allowed into temples. The law does not allow such discrimination, but people with powerful backing from higher-caste Hindus do not allow Dalits into temples. In many villages, the Dalits are not allowed to draw water from the wells used by higher-caste Hindus. In many villages, the higher-caste Hindus with influence and money power don't allow the Dalits to enjoy their economic gains in the form of better marriage or social functions. Still, the children of higher-caste Hindus are going to be a happy lot. They will have no complaints that a Dalit with a low rank got into a government job or a government college or school.

Many Hindus belonging to higher castes as well as backward classes or even lower castes have developed certain institutions to help the students and the people of their caste with funds from the well-to-do sections of their caste along with some help from the government in the form of allocation of land. Once the caste system is abolished, there is going to be a problem in running these institutions. Generally, these caste-based institutions bear the name of the caste or subcaste it belongs to, and the entry or benefit is first for their own caste. Once the caste system is abolished, the Maha Mandir cannot allow these institutions to use the name of their caste in the title. The Maha Mandir also cannot permit these caste-based institutions to admit only the students of a particular caste or to grant benefits only to a particular caste.

The Maha Mandir has to take the administration of all the caste-based institution under its fold. All the Hindu temples are going to be under the umbrella of the Maha Mandir, so there is no reason why all caste-based institutions cannot be under the Maha Mandir. Perhaps that is the best way in the absence of any other solution. It is going to benefit the whole Hindu society.

The best solution will be to allow all the Hindus, irrespective of their castes, into boarding dharamshalas, marriage halls, and all such institutions. The management may remain with the promoters, but the Maha Mandir must monitor the workings of these institutions to see that there is no caste-based discrimination. Another point is that many such institutions were promoted or created three to six decades back or even a century back. Now the land of these institutions is priced in crores of rupees. All these institutions come under the purview of the charity commissioner of the related area. The management of such institutions do not permit its relocation to new areas, nor does the charity commissioner have any power to do so. The Maha Mandir can take action to either relocate certain institutions or even abandon them. The relocation can generate crores of rupees to the exchequer of Maha Mandir.

Once the caste system is abolished, the biggest problem going to be faced by Hindus is in their matrimonial affairs. At present, more than 90 per cent of marriages in India are arranged; the percentage in rural areas is even higher. The Chinese Communist Party had discouraged the system of arranged marriages in the 1940s and in later decades. The same is not possible in India.

While going for an arranged marriage the Indian parents first look for the caste of the groom or bride in question. Presently, there are tens of matrimonial portals serving the needs of urban match seekers. The texts of all the matrimonial advertisements have caste mentioned in them. Once the caste system is abolished, the Maha Mandir cannot allow the match seekers to mention their former castes in their matrimonial advertisements. The solution to this problem is that the match seekers must mention the economic class they belong to, maybe middle income, higher middle income. Some people may mention a specific monthly or yearly income of the groom in such advertisements, which is the practice even now.

In late 1950s, the metric system in weights, measurements, and currency was introduced. People were barred from mentioning old terms while mentioning the details about their products or goods. There was penalty if they did so. This law continues even today. Similarly, the Maha Mandir can impose penalty if match seekers mention their former caste in matrimonial advertisements.

It is going to be a very long time before people will start marrying into castes other than their own. Nothing stops them from talking about their caste in person and then deciding accordingly. Still slowly, the abolition of the caste system will have an impact on arranged marriages. Such marriages are already on the rise in urban areas.

Old habits die hard. The caste system has been prevailing in Hinduism for thousands of years. Hinduism is mainly based on mythology, and all the texts of mythological stories mention the higher castes showing hatred towards the lower castes. These notions, which are thousands of years old, are not going to vanish overnight, but maybe in ten to twenty years, they can. The younger generation of so-called higher-caste Hindus is going to feel happy with the abolition of the caste system. They are not going to complain about their job going to a person in lower rank or their admission in a college or school going to a candidate with much lower marks. The people from scheduled castes, scheduled tribes are going to feel happy with higher disposal income in their hands in lieu of an illusionary government job in addition to the restoration of their self-esteem before the higher-caste Hindus.

Initially, there is going to be some chaos in rural areas once the caste system is abolished. The old people from higher castes may not be able to digest the new development and resist treating the Dalits at par with them. The Maha Mandir, on its part, has to educate the Dalits to adopt better hygiene and cleanliness practices if they want to be accepted by the higher-class Hindus.

The Maha Mandir can stop the entry in temples of any person with filth irrespective of his caste.

The Likely Opposition to the Abolition of the Caste System

When all is said and done, a five-thousand-year-old practice cannot be done away so easily by the Maha Mandir. There is likely to be a strong opposition from the Dalit leaders in the country.

There is no doubt that in past, for thousands of years, the Dalits have been subjected to very inhumane treatment by the higher-caste Hindus. The Dalit leaders may argue that a period of seventy years is a small period, considering the agony faced by the Dalits for thousands of years. During the seventy years of independence, the economic condition at large has not improved for them. They have a point, but their argument should not stop the Maha Mandir from eradicating the caste system from Hinduism.

As discussed earlier, switching over to the direct transfer of funds to the bank accounts of poor and other underprivileged classes is a prerequisite before the abolition of the caste system from Hinduism. Presently, there are about 15 crores families in the segments of very poor, poor, and lower middle income groups. If an amount of Rs.20,000 per annum is transferred to the bank account of such families, the annual burden on the government is going to be 3 lakh crores. India's current GDP is about 140 lakh crores, and the taxes collected by the central government and the state governments reach to about 24 lakhs crores, which is 17 per cent of the GDP.

There have been talks of direct fund transfers to the bank accounts of the poor and underprivileged families in India for a long time now. In fact, it is the standard practice adopted by bulk by developing countries throughout the world. The leakages due to corruption come down if the funds are directly transferred to the beneficiaries' accounts in comparison to the present system of subsidies in prices of food grains and items for general consumption.

A solution to the problem of further obtaining a level playing field for the Dalits is that the Dalit families can be given a benefit of 50 per cent more amount in their bank accounts for a period of ten years or more as agreed by the government. Out of 15 crores beneficiary families for the direct transfer of funds, the Dalit families are supposed to account for 50 per cent of them, or 7.5 crores families. If an amount of Rs.30,000 per annum is deposited into the accounts of these Dalit families instead of Rs.20,000, the total outgo will increase to 3.75 lakh crores from 3 lakh crores.

There is nothing wrong if the government spends Rs.75,000 crores per annum to satisfy the former Dalits. This kind of arrangement will not stop the Maha Mandir from eradicating the caste system from Hinduism. The direct fund transfers should take place only after the caste system is gone. Once it happens, the new beneficiaries should be treated as former Dalits. There should not be any problem in defining the Dalit families, and the benefits should go to all the Dalit families irrespective of their economic strata.

A 50 per cent more amount in the bank accounts of Dalits in comparison to others should be treated as compensation to them from other Hindu castes that have exploited and insulted them for centuries. This arrangement must satisfy the Dalit leaders, and there should not be any hindrance for the Maha Mandir to eradicate the caste system.

Cow Protection: A Challenge for the Maha Mandir

The great Mahatma Gandhi believed that the central fact of Hinduism is cow protection. He advocated that cow protection in Hinduism was a symbol of animal rights and of non-violence against all life forms. He venerated cows and suggested ending cow slaughter to be the first step in stopping violence against all animals. He said that he will worship it and shall defend his stand against the whole world.

Perhaps it was Mahatma Gandhi whose views on cow protection had a great influence on the Constitution of India, which came into effect in early 1950. The framers of the Constitution of India declared India as a secular state, but the term *secular* did not appear anywhere in the document. Interestingly, the constitution couched the protection of Hinduism's sacred animal in the modernist language of science, not in religious terms. Since then, the legal battle over cow protection has shifted to state legislations and the courts. Now only a few Indian states allow cow slaughter with certain restrictions. There is no national ban on cow slaughter; still, majority of states feature statewide legislation criminalizing cow slaughter and beef consumption.

As per the old Hindu texts, only the Kshatriya community was allowed to raise arms in case of any internal or external conflict. Still as per Hindu texts, the Brahmans could raise arms if there was an attack on sacred cows. This fact shows the importance of cow protection in Hinduism.

With Maha Mandir, the apex Hindu body, in place, it is going to be imperative that all matters related to cow protection is handled by the apex religious body and not by state governments. It will help the central government and all the state government to devote all their time and energy on governance rather than indulging petty matters related to cow protection.

Before moving further on the subject of cow protection, it is necessary for the readers to know about the modern-day practices in some other Asian countries.

In Nepal, the cow is the national animal. People consider cow like the goddess Lakshmi, goddess of wealth and prosperity. During Diwali, the Nepalese perform prayers for sacred cows. Significantly, Nepal has been the only Hindu kingdom on earth for centuries. Lately, in 2015 the new Constitution of Nepal talks about the secularism ending the Hindu state status of Nepal. Maybe in the coming years, Nepal may relax its strict rules on cow protection.

In Myanmar, beef taboo is fairly widespread, particularly in the Buddhist community. In Myanmar, beef is typically obtained from cattle that are slaughtered at the end of their working lives (maybe at sixteen years of age) or from sick animals. Few people eat beef, and there is general dislike of beef.

In Sri Lanka, the Buddhist community greatly believes in non-violence against animals. Still religious minorities are allowed to slaughter cows. There are protests going on by the Buddhist monks against cow slaughter.

In China, Buddhism, Confucianism, and Daoism all share the idea of state protection of cows, but neither cow slaughter nor beef consumption is banned. Recently, China has become a growing market for beef imported from USA. The Chinese are supposed to be mad for pork, but the demand for beef is now growing fast.

In ancient Japan, because of Buddhist influence, historically there was beef taboo. Slaughtering of most of the animals was banned till 1872. Later, it was officially proclaimed that the emperor of Japan consumed beef and mutton. It transformed the country's dietary considerations as a means of modernizing the country, particularly with regard to consumption of beef.

The readers also ought to know that for a dairy farmer, the cow is useful as long as it yields milk. Once it goes dry, what is a dairy farmer going to do with it? The cost of feeding each animal is roughly Rs.100 per day. Earnings from a barren animal is zero. Selling it for slaughter would fetch Rs.15,000 to Rs.20,000 per head of cattle.

Now with around 80 per cent of the Indian states banning cow slaughter, dairy farmers have no option but to let barren cows roam free and forage for whatever they can find to eat. The feral cows now barge into cropland, eating whatever crops are growing. The farmers are furious at the new source of pestilence. Dairy farmers throw up their hands and say that they have no option but to let dry cattle forage for themselves. Both are correct; it's a losing proposition for everyone.

In cities and towns, the barren cows roam around freely, sometimes hurting people, particularly two-wheeler riders and the pedestrians. On a highway, a roaming cow can cause an accident by suddenly coming before a speeding car. In monsoon times, whenever there is a dry spell, hundreds of cows sit on roads in towns and cities, slowing down the traffic movement. Many such cows harass the fruits and vegetable vendors and eat into their potential daily earning. The vendors find themselves simply helpless before the strong lobbies of dairy farmers and so-called cow protectors.

The readers should also take a note that most of the dairy farmers do not sell out their barren cows, but still many sell their cows to slaughterers at whatever price they can get. Many sell them to gangs of people who smuggle the cows to Bangladesh through an organized network. These smugglers sometimes also steal the free-roaming barren cows and send them out of the country. The owners or dairy farmers don't complain. In fact, a part of the economy of Bangladesh thrives on cows smuggled from India.

Till now there is no Hindu apex authority in place. The right wing Bharatiya Janata Party has been championing the cause of cow protection. Many antisocial elements as well as overenthusiastic Hindus have been creating trouble for the government as well as the common men. The Apex Hindu authority, the Maha Mandir, once in place, must come forward and take over the responsibility of cow protection, which is the core idea of Hinduism.

Rs.100 per day is needed to feed a barren or dry cow which has been abandoned by a dairy farmer. In addition, approximately Rs.50 per day is needed for the cost of sheltering a cow and for the staff expenses to maintain the shelters. India today has an estimated population of 24 million barren, or dry, cows. If a cost of Rs.55,000 per annum is considered to feed and shelter a dry cow, the cost of protecting 24 million cows throughout India is going to be a whopping 1.35 lakhs crores, which is almost 1 per cent of India's present GDP.

A sobering fact is that almost 25 per cent of barren cows are looked after by the *panjrapoles*, which are run by the Jain community, till their death. It still leaves a figure of 18 million cows requiring protection and care by the Hindu community. There are 200 million Hindu families in India against the figure of 18 million dry cows. The amount required to be spent by an average Hindu family on cow protection throughout India comes to about Rs.5,000 per annum or about Rs.14 per day per Hindu family.

Many Hindus—particularly, the Hindu leaders—express their views on the protection of cows, saying, 'The cow is our mother.' Do we kill our parents when they stop working or when they are of no use? So whatever it may cost, we must protect the cows. Often the PM Mr Modi requests the people not to indulge in any violence while protecting the cows. He has always emphasized that the cows must be protected, and there is no doubt about that. He echoes the views expressed by Mahatma Gandhi a century back.

The newly formed Hindu apex body, the Maha Mandir, must respect the common sentiment of all Hindus, who are now in excess of a billion in population. At the same time, the apex body must enlighten the Hindus about the enormous costs of cow protection and the fact that it is the duty of all Hindus to bear the cost for cow protection. India after all is a secular country, and the Hindus should not expect the government to spend on cow protection. The government has to spend on general infrastructure for roads, transportation, communication, electricity, education, healthcare, and industries in addition to expenses on maintenance of law and order and social welfare programmes.

When we talk about the protection of cows, it has to be in toto. We the Hindus cannot afford to allow the sacred cows to roam free on roads and block the traffic or hurt the two-wheeler riders and pedestrians. We can also not allow our mother cows to eat all the dirty things and plastic materials. We can also not allow them to get into the fields of vegetable growers or eat the stuff of poor vegetable and fruit vendors.

The cost of cow protection is enormous. There cannot be going back or saving on cost by any means. A cow needs more than Rs.100 per day to feed, no amount can be saved on that. Simultaneously, all the cows need shelter, and that is the only way to keep them away from roaming freely on roads in urban areas or the fields in rural areas. A cow on average needs an area of 50 square feet for shelter, and at the most, an employee can take care of 25 cows under him. India needs about 900 million square feet of space to shelter 18 million abandoned dry cows. There's also no amount that can be saved on sheltering cows. A space of 900 million square feet in the rural area is enough to accommodate more than 2 million rural families belonging to poor class. A recent study puts the space occupied by each poor rural family at around 425 square feet. So a space of 900 million square feet shall deprive more than 2 million poor families in rural areas from having their residential accommodation.

The silver lining of the cow protection campaign is going to be the employment it is going to generate. More than 7 lakhs persons shall be needed to look after 18 million cows since, on an average, a person can look after about 25 cows. Here also there is no chance of saving.

As mentioned earlier, like the Hindu community, the Jain community also has deep faith in cows. The Jains call the cow shelters by the name panjrapole. These panjrapoles are generally located in the heart of cities and are taking care of almost 20 per cent of cows abandoned by dairy farmers all over India. There are other social organizations also sheltering cows and taking care of a further 5 per cent of abandoned cows. There are many dairy farmers who deposit their abandoned cows with either a panjrapole or some other cow shelter along with a lump sum payment towards the maintenance of that cow for a certain period. The Maha Mandir must praise the job done by the Jain community as well as some other social organizations.

Since India is a secular country, the amount of Rs.1 lakh crores has to come from the Hindu families only and not from the government.

The readers ought to know that there are over 11 crores of elders in India in the age group of sixty plus, and the number is going up very fast. Out of the 11 crores of such elders, there are more than nine crores of elders who don't enjoy any pension benefit from their previous employer's pension fund. They either continue to work for their survival or depend on their family members to look after them. The state governments provide a pension to elders, ranging from Rs.6,000 to Rs.18,000 per annum. This is much lower than the funds of Rs.55,000 per cow needed for the protection of barren cows.

The readers also ought to know that the allocation of funds by the Indian government for the education and healthcare sectors every year is far below than the funds spent by other developing countries in ratio of their GDP. The result is that there are not enough teachers and other staff. Many employed teachers and staff are also absent every day. The school buildings are in poor shape, and the education imparted by the government schools and colleges is very poor. The government is forced to compel the private schools to accommodate the students from the poor classes to the tune of 25 per cent of their strength. Nowhere in the world has such a practice prevailed.

The healthcare sector is also in shambles. There is great shortage of doctors and nurses. The hospitals are not well equipped. Sometimes the medicines are in shortage, or the medicines in store in a hospital have expired.

There is no doubt that 1 billion Hindus in India have deep faith in cows. They consider the cow as their mother and worship it. But India does not belong to Hindus only. It is a secular country. The Hindus must spend from their own pockets for cow protection, and it will strengthen their self-respect and self-esteem. Nobody in the world is going to ask his neighbour to look after his mother if he is competent enough to do so himself. The government should not spend on cow protection and should concentrate more on funding education and healthcare.

There are more than 20 crores Hindu families in India who are required to spend Rs.1 lakh crores per annum on cow protection. The amount comes to less than Rs.5,000 per family per annum. If we seek total cow protection in our country, we have to manage these funds. Cow protection should not be partial where some cows are sheltered and fed well while others are left to roam free or where some are allowed to reach slaughterhouses while some are smuggled to Bangladesh through a network of dubious people.

How is the money going to come for the task of cow protection to the tune of Rs.1 lakh crores every year? The task is difficult—easier said than done. The newly formed Maha Mandir has to look into it. There can be either full cow protection or no cow protection at all. All Hindu families have to understand the gravity of this task.

The Maha Mandir would do well to direct all the Hindu temples under its fold to forward all the money received to the cow protection fund managed by it. Many priests of some Hindu temples lead a lavish lifestyle. They should be asked to give it up for the sake of cow protection. Many Hindu temples serve free meals to their devotees every day and also provide night accommodation at a very nominal cost or for free. All this shall have to be stopped. The temples should charge a reasonable cost for the meals as well as night stay and forward the amount received to Maha Mandir's cow protection fund. The devotees shall not mind paying once they know that the amount goes to cow protection. Alternatively, the temples can stop free meals and forward the money saved to the cow protection fund. The space occupied by the rooms for night stay can be altered to shelter cows.

On many festivals, tens of thousands of people go to a certain temple. There are many donors arranging free meals for them on their way to the temple. These free meals have to be stopped, and the funds saved have to go directly to the cow protection fund. At the same time, all devotees from the poor section of society have to be requested and educated by Maha Mandir not to donate even a single rupee to any temple or Hindu religious place. These poor people can use the money saved on better feeding, education, and healthcare of their children. Practically, the funds used for the benefit of the poor section of society by certain donors shall go directly to the cow protection fund, and poor people will not donate to temples.

There is an increasing trend of padayatra by devotees throughout the country. A group of people commences a padayatra to reach a temple on a certain week or a certain festival. Many Hindu donors come up to help the pilgrims and offer free meals on their way to the temple. This kind of practice not only creates obstacles for the traffic on highways; it also occupies space for the provision of free meals. It also creates an unhygienic atmosphere on the road. A close scrutiny will reveal that most of the *padyatris* are from the poor section of society. The donors take pride in that they are helping them, but they don't know many of these people take up padayatra only because of the free meals available and to run away from their regular employment or work.

If free meals are stopped on the way of a padayatra, the money saved can go to the cow protection fund. The padyatris also shall benefit because they will be concentrating on their work to earn a living. This kind of bitter pill is something only the Maha Mandir can prescribe. Neither the government nor the politicians can do so.

In monsoon times, particularly in northern India, there are Kavadiyas taking up padyatras in groups on roads leading to Ganga River to take holy Ganga water and then bring it back to particular temples. Here also many donors come forward and help them. Many times, these Kavadiyas block the traffic on highways. A close scrutiny will reveal that many of them are unsocial elements. The practice is tens of decades old but has to be stopped by the Maha Mandir.

The donors in northern India compete among themselves to help and serve these Kavadiyas on their way to Ganga as well as when they come back. Their night stay is arranged by the donors and bhajans and kirtans are played over noisy, loud speakers. Many times the bhajans are based on songs from Hindi movies; sometimes they play vulgar songs. Many Kavadiyas consume drugs and alcohol during the night; still they are well fed and served.

The Maha Mandir must stop the practice of the Kavadiyas. It cannot be allowed in modern times. In advanced countries, the pedestrians are not allowed on highways. They are fined if they do so. The Kavadiyas obstruct the traffic in a big way, and the people tolerate it in the name of faith. Sometimes, if a Kavadiya is hurt by a vehicle, all the Kavadiyas get to together and burn many vehicles. The Maha Mandir should not tolerate this kind of practice.

In old times, life was slow. The Hindu month of Shraavan falls in the monsoon season. It's the month between the sowing and reaping of crops. The rural people related to farming activities is somewhat free during this period. The practice of the Kavadiyas developed in the past due to lesser farming activity during the month of Shraavan and deep faith in the water of Ganga, which is supposed to be poured on Shivling. The Hindus took it as a holy act.

Life is no slower during the twenty-first century. Highways by global standards have been developed, and kilometres of highways are going to be added in the coming years. All the villages are also being connected by roads to these national and state highways. The roads and highways are meant for the speedy traffic of vehicles. The Kavadiyas cannot be allowed to create obstacles for a month to the movement of vehicles. A close scrutiny will reveal that more than half of the Kavadiyas belong to the very poor class, and they don't like to work. They are happy to get free food and all kinds of services from the donors during their journey to the Ganga and back to temples.

The Maha Mandir shall be doing a great service to the society and even Kavadiyas by stopping this practice. The money saved by the donors should be diverted to the cow protection fund. The move will help in a big way to the speedy movement of traffic in northern India during the Hindu month of Shraavan. Many human lives also will be saved. This kind of action cannot be expected from the society or the politicians.

There are hundreds of ashrams run by certain self-proclaimed god-men, gurus, and babas throughout

India. These ashrams occupy thousands of acres of land allotted by the state governments free of cost or at a very nominal lease amount. The Maha Mandir has to take all these ashrams in its fold and govern them. Some of the gurus have properties in the form of ashrams worth hundreds of crores, because these ashrams are a part of urban areas and the prices of land have increased manifold during the last two decades.

The Maha Mandir should see to it that the incomes generated by these ashrams go to the cow protection fund after allowing for all reasonable expenses, like maintenance costs. Many god-men and gurus lead a lavish life and have a team of sevaks working for them. The Maha Mandir should see to it that the operating cost of an ashram comes down and that the money saved is routed to the cow protection fund.

In certain cases, the Maha Mandir will find that there is a lot of additional land in an ashram. The Maha Mandir should seek permission from the charity commissioner and should sell the additional land and remit the payment to the cow protection fund. Certain ashrams provide free meals to visitors and also provide free night stay to them. The ashram should start charging and divert the money to the Maha Mandir.

The Maha Mandir should create a model ashram so that it occupies minimum land. The purpose of an ashram is to have spiritual discourses for the Hindus. A discourse needs a place that can accommodate the amount of people attending it. A spiritual guru may have a large following and need a large auditorium to address them. The Maha Mandir can decide on the matter, whether an ashram should offer meals to the visitors or accommodation for the stay of guests. In the old times, the ashrams were located far away from urban areas, and the visitors could not get meals around them as well as any housing accommodation. The same is not the case in modern times. Food is offered by the ashrams to increase their influence on the devotees. The accommodation to stay is also offered for the same reason. The Maha Mandir can decide on stopping the facility and selling the additional space occupied by such facilities. The money received by selling such additional spaces can be transferred to the cow protection fund.

In certain cases, if an ashram is located in a rural area and has lot of additional land, the land can be used to shelter a number of cows. To sum up, ashrams can be useful in generating funds for cow protection.

The Ayurveda, yoga, Vastu Shastra, and Jyotish Shastra are the branches of Hinduism. Any person involved in manufacturing Ayurveda medicines should be made responsible to contribute certain amount of profit generated to the cow protection fund. Similarly, persons who make profits from teaching yoga should be made responsible to contribute some of their profits to the cow protection fund. There are many persons involved in guiding people on Vastushastra. They charge very high fees. They should be made to pay certain amount of profits to the cow protection fund. There is no reason why the astrologers practising Hindu Jyotish Shastra should not contribute some of their profits to the cow protection fund.

An amount of Rs.1 lakh crores per annum required for the cow protection is a huge sum. The Maha Mandir has to find some innovative ideas to generate the funds. Cow protection is related to the deep faith of Hindus in cows. The Maha Mandir can appeal to all the Hindus who can afford it to donate generously to the cow protection fund on birthdays of their near and dear ones as well as marriages in their family.

There are more than 10 million weddings taking place in India every year. Almost one third of them belong to middle class, upper middle class, rich, and super rich people. By a wild guestimate, an average amount spent by this affluent section of people on a wedding comes to about Rs.1 million. The Maha Mandir can appeal to this affluent section to donate 5 per cent of the amount of their expenditure on the weddings to the cow protection fund. It will immensely help the cause of cow protection.

Future Scenario of Cow Protection

As discussed earlier, the cost of cow protection is a whopping Rs.1 lakh crores per annum, and there is no scope for any compromise on such expenditure. There is an increasing awareness among Hindus about the cow protection, particularly with the female members of every Hindu family. All of them agree that the cows must be protected as per the belief of Hinduism. But till now the cost occurring in the task of cow protection has not been worked out by any group or any political party or the media. Once the cow lovers come to know about the whopping cost of Rs.1 lakh crores per annum, some of them are definitely going to develop cold feet.

At present, there are 110 million people in India in the age group of 60 plus. By 2030 the figure will likely be 200 million. The Indian government supports more than 80 per cent of elders who have worked in unorganized sector by a paltry pension ranging between Rs.500 to Rs.1,500 per month. The cost of cow protection is going to be around Rs.4,500 per month. The awareness in young generation Hindus about cow protection is very low. At present, they may not object to the whopping cost on cow protection, but later on, when they grow up, maybe by 2025, they are surely going to object. They are not going to digest the fact that our elders don't get the desired attention and treatment in their old age and that we do a lot of spending on barren cows.

When we talk about the cow protection, we try to imitate the neighbouring country Nepal. For centuries, Nepal has been recognized throughout the world in the past as the only Hindu kingdom on earth. Many Indian Hindus are not fully aware about the fact that Nepal is no longer a Hindu kingdom but a secular democratic country. The cow continues to be the national animal of Nepal, but sooner or later, Nepal may partially relax the ban on cow slaughter as well as the consumption of beef, keeping in tune with secularism. Recently, the leftist parties have succeeded in forming the government of Nepal and have little faith in any religion.

In India, few people are aware about the historical fact that love and respect for cows among Hindus have paved the way for Muslim invaders about a thousand years back. The Muslim invaders during those days used to keep a horde of cows as a shield during war so the Hindus could not defend themselves, as they could not kill the cows. The funny thing is that the Hindus today try to keep Muslims away from slaughtering the cows and consuming the beef. Maybe they want to settle the account by doing so. What the Hindus have not been aware of is the whopping cost of cow protection.

It is also a funny matter that India is following as a model a poor tiny neighbour. Nepal may also be abandoned in the future because it is now a secular country. Before going for complete action on cow protection, the Maha Mandir must take into account the practices in Buddhist countries. Buddhism has belief similar to Hinduism on any violence against animals, but the countries with a Buddhist majority also are not able to follow all the norms to fulfil their belief.

The Maha Mandir should also consider the fact that in spite of its best and sincere efforts, total cow protection cannot be achieved. Some cows are going to reach the slaughterhouses, and many of them are going to be smuggled to the neighbouring Bangladesh. The problem of stray cows will still persist in both urban and rural areas but may be in lower numbers.

Still the Maha Mandir has to take the task of cow protection in an earnest manner. It cannot be left to the government since India is a secular country and only the Hindus are supposed to spend on their belief and faith. Let the future generation of Hindus decide whether to continue the practice of cow protection and go on spending an amount in excess of Rs.1 lakh crores.

Hindu Organization

*H*induism, being the oldest religion on earth, has existed since more than five thousand years but without an apex body as well as apex head. Many outsiders have intruded into the Indian land but have not succeeded in converting the Hindus at large into their religion. A few have accepted Islam as their religion, and less than them accepted Christianity as their religion. Hindus take pride in that in spite of all that's happening, their religion has held intact against all the odds. The strange thing is that the Dalits have stayed in the Hindu fold in spite of all inhumane treatment to them by Hindus from other castes during all these five thousand years.

A few notable Hindu organizations came up during the twentieth century—namely, Akhil Bharatiya Hindu Mahasabha, Rashtriya Swayamsevak Sangh, Vishva Hindu Parishad, and Bajrang Dal. Prior to formation of these Hindu organizations, Akhil Bharatiya Akhara Parishad has existed for centuries. Adi Shankaracharya is known to have established seven *akharas*—or as some say ten akharas—as far back as early eight century. The

Akhil Bharatiya Akhara Parishad occasionally comes in the limelight when the Kumbh Melas are held at Allahabad, Nasik, and Ujjain.

Akhil Bharatiya Hindu Mahasabha

It was founded in 1915 by Madan Mohan Malviya and is a right wing Hindu nationalist political party in India. The organization was formed to protect the rights of the Hindu community in British India after the formation of All-India Muslim League in 1906 and the British India government's creation of separate Muslim electorate under the Morley–Minto reforms of 1909. Although quite an old Hindu nationalist party, the Hindu Mahasabha has remained marginal in its influence on Indian politics, both before and after independence.

In 1909, Arya Samaj leaders Lala Lajpat Rai, Lala Chand, and Shadi Lal established Punjab Hindu Sabha (assembly). Madan Mohan Malviya presided over the *sabha*'s first session at Lahore in October 1909. The sabha stated that it was not a sectarian organization but an 'all-embracing movement' that aimed to safeguard the interests of 'the entire Hindu community'. On 21– 22 October 1909, it organized the Punjab Provincial Hindu Conference, which criticized the Indian National Congress for failing to defend Hindu interests and called for promotion of Hindu-centred politics. The sabha organized five more annual provincial conferences in Punjab.

The development of the broad work for Hindu unity that started in the early twentieth century in Punjab was the precursor for the formation of the All-India Hindu Sabha. Over the next few years, several such Hindu sabhas were established outside Punjab, including in the

United Provinces, Bihar, Bengal, Central Provinces and Berar, and Bombay presidency.

A formal move to establish an umbrella All-India Sabha was made at the Allahabad session of congress in 1910. A committee headed by Lala Baijnath was set up to draw up a constitution, but it did not make much progress. Another conference of Hindu leaders in Allahabad also took the initial step to establish an all-India Hindu sabha in 1910, but this organization did not become operational due to factional strife. On 8 December 1913, the Punjab Hindu Sabha passed a resolution to create an All-India Hindu Sabha at its Ambala session. The conference proposed holding general conferences of Hindu leaders from all over India at the 1915 Kumbh Mela in Haridwar.

Preparatory sessions of the All-India Hindu Sabha were held at Haridwar (13 February 1915), Lucknow (17 February 1915), and Delhi (27 February 1915). In April 1915, Sarvadeshak (All-India) Hindu Sabha was formed as an umbrella organization of regional Hindu sabhas at the Kumbh Mela in Haridwar. Gandhi and Swami Shraddhanand were also present at the conference and were supportive of the formation of the All-India Hindu Sabha. The sabha laid emphasis on Hindu solidarity and the need for social reform. Manindra Chandra Nandy, the president of the conference, declared that the sabha would be loyal to the British government. This pro-British stance was criticized by Shraddhanand.

The sabha formally changed its name of Akhil Bharatiya (all-India) Hindu Mahasabha at its sixth session in April 1921. Presided over by Manindra Chandra Nandy, it amended its constitution to remove the clause about loyalty to the British and added a clause committing the organization to a 'united and self-governing' Indian nation.

Among the Mahasabha's early leaders was the prominent nationalist and educationalist Pandit Madan Mohan Malviya, who founded the Banaras Hindu University, and the Punjabi populist Lala Lajpat Rai. Under Malviya, the Mahasabha campaigned for Hindu political unity, for the education and economic development of Hindus, as well as for the conversion of Muslims to Hinduism.

In the late 1920s, the Mahasabha came under the influence of leaders like Balakrishna Shivram Moonje and Vinayak Damodar Savarkar. Savarkar was a former revolutionary who had been banned from anti-British political activities and opposed the secularism of the congress. Under Savarkar, the Mahasabha became a more intense critic of the congress and its policy of wooing Muslim support. The Mahasabha suffered a setback when in 1925, its former member Keshav Baliram Hedgewar left to form the Rashtriya Swayamsevak Sangh, a Hindu volunteer organization that abstained from active politics. Although ideologically similar to the Mahasabha, the RSS grew faster across the nation and became a competitor for the core constituency of the Mahasabha.

The Hindu Mahasabha did not actively support the Indian freedom movement against the British rule in India, nor was it exactly loyal to the British Raj. After the formation of Rashtriya Swayamsevak Sangh, the Hindu Mahasabha rapidly lost its importance and was marginalized in Indian politics.

Rashtriya Swayamsevak Sangh

It was founded on September 27, 1925, by Shri Keshav Baliram Hedgewar, a former member of Hindu Mahasabha. It is a sort of right wing volunteer paramilitary organization with a purpose of spreading the Hindutva and Hindu nationalism. It has its headquarters based at Nagpur, Maharashtra. It has to its credit about 5–6 million volunteers and more than 56,000 shakhas spread all over India. The Bharatiya Janata Party, the ruling party at the centre as well as in many states, is the political wing of RSS. Akhil Bharatiya Vidyarthi Parishad is the student wing of RSS, and Bharatiya Mazdoor Sangh is the labour union affiliated to RSS.

The RSS is going to be a great asset under its fold for the Maha Mandir, and it is going to be a big challenge too for it, considering the huge experience and strength of RSS.

Claiming a commitment to selfless service to the nation, the RSS is world's largest voluntary missionary organization.

The initial impetus was to provide character training through Hindu discipline and to unite the Hindu community to form a Hindu *rashtra* (Hindu nation). The organization promotes the ideals of upholding Indian culture and the values of civil society and propagates the ideology of Hindutva, to strengthen the majority of the Hindu community. It drew initial inspiration from European right wing groups during World War II. Gradually, RSS grew into a prominent Hindu nationalist umbrella organization, spawning several affiliated organizations that established numerous schools, charities, and clubs to spread its ideological beliefs.

The RSS was banned once during the British rule and then thrice by the post-independence Indian government—first in 1948 when a former RSS member assassinated Mahatma Gandhi, then during the emergency (1975–77), and for a third time, after the demolition of Babri Masjid in 1992.

The founder of RSS, Hedgewar, believed that a handful of British were able to rule over the vast country of India because Hindus were disunited, lacked valour (*prarkram*), and lacked civic character. He recruited energetic Hindu youth with revolutionary fervour and gave them a uniform (black forage cap, khaki shirt (later white shirt), and khaki shorts)—emulating the British police—and taught them paramilitary techniques with *lathi* (bamboo staff), sword, javelin, and dagger. Hindu ceremonies and rituals played a large role in the organization, not so much for religious observance, but to provide awareness of India's glorious past and to bind the members in a religious communion. Hedgewar also held weekly sessions of what he called *baudhik* (ideological education), which consisted of simple questions to the novices concerning the Hindu nation and its history and heroes, especially Shivaji. The saffron flag of Shivaji, the Bhagwa Dhwaj, was used as the emblem for the new organization. Its public tasks involved protecting Hindu pilgrims at festivals and confronting Muslim resistance against Hindu processions near mosques.

Two years into the life of the organization, in 1927, Hedgewar organized an officers' training camp with the objective of forming a corps of key workers, whom he called *pracharaks*. He asked the volunteers to become sadhus first, renouncing professional and family lives and dedicating themselves to the cause of the RSS. According to scholar Christophe Jaffrelot, Hedgewar embraced this doctrine after it had been reinterpreted by militant nationalists, such as Aurobindo. The tradition of renunciation gave the RSS the character of a Hindu sect. Development of the shakha network of the RSS was the main preoccupation for Hedgewar throughout his career as the RSS chief. The first pracharaks were responsible for establishing as many shakhas as possible, first, in Nagpur, then across Maharashtra, and eventually in the rest of India. P. B. Dani was sent to establish a shakha at the Banaras Hindu University, and other universities were similarly targeted for recruitment of new followers from the student population.

After the formation of the RSS, which portrayed itself as a social movement, Hedgewar kept the organization from having any direct affiliation with the political organizations then fighting British rule, but he and his team of volunteers did take part in the Indian National Congress and led movements against the British rule. Hedgewar was arrested in the Jungle Satyagraha agitation in 1931 and served a second term in prison. RSS rejected Gandhi's willingness to cooperate with the Muslims.

In accordance with the Hedgewar's tradition of keeping the RSS away from the Indian independence movement, any political activity that could be construed as being anti-British was carefully avoided. According to the RSS biographer, C. P. Bhishikar, Hedgewar talked only about Hindu organizations, avoiding any direct comment on the government. The 'independence day' announced by the Indian National Congress for 26 January 1930 was celebrated by the RSS only that year and was subsequently avoided. The tricolour of the Indian national movement was shunned. Hedgewar personally participated in the *satyagraha* launched by Gandhi in April 1930, but he did not get the RSS involved in the movement. He sent information everywhere that the RSS would not participate in the satyagraha. However, those wishing to participate individually were not prohibited.

Golwalkar, who became the leader of the RSS in 1940, continued and further strengthened the isolation from the independence movement. In his view, the RSS had pledged to achieve freedom through 'defending religion and culture' and not by fighting the British.

Golwalkar even lamented the anti-British nationalism, calling it a reactionary view that had disastrous effects upon the entire course of the freedom struggle. It is believed that Golwalkar did not want to give the British any excuse to ban the RSS. He compiled with all the strictures imposed by the government during the Second World War, even announcing the termination of the RSS military department. The British government stated that the RSS was not at all supporting any civil disobedience against them and as such their other political activities could be overlooked. The British Home Department took note of the fact that the speakers at the sangh meetings urged its members to keep aloof from the anti-British movements of the Indian National Congress; this instruction was duly followed. The Home Department was thereby of the opinion that the RSS did not constitute a menace to the law and order in British India. The Bombay government, in a report, appreciated the RSS by noting that the sangh had scrupulously kept itself within the law and refrained from taking part in Quit India Movement that broke out in August 1942.

The partition of India affected millions of Sikhs, Hindus, and Muslims attempting to escape the violence and carnage that followed. During partition, RSS helped the Hindus and Sikhs refugees from West Punjab, and its activists also played a very active role in the communal violence during the Hindu–Muslim riots in North India, though this was officially not sanctioned by the leadership. To the RSS activists, the partition was a result of mistaken soft line towards the Muslims by the congress party.

The Rashtriya Swayamsevak Sangh initially did not recognize the tricolour as the national flag of India. The RSS mouthpiece, the *Organiser*, in its issue dated 17 July 1947, demanded, in an editorial titled 'National Flag', that the Bhagwa Dwaj (saffron flag) be adopted as the national flag of India. The tricolour was adopted as the national flag of India by the Constituent Assembly of India on 22 July 1947. The RSS hoisted the national flag of India at its headquarters in Nagpur on 14 August 1947 and on 26 January 1950 but stopped doing so after that. This issue has always been a source of controversy.

The Rashtriya Swayamsevak Sangh initially did not recognize the Constitution of India, strongly criticizing it because the Constitution of India made no mention of the Laws of Manu, from the controversial ancient Hindu text Manu-smriti, which had been said to denigrate the lower castes and untouchables of India.

Following Mahatma Gandhi's assassination in January 1948 by a former member of RSS, Nathuram Godse, many prominent leaders of the RSS were arrested, and RSS as an organization was banned on 4 February 1948. A commission of inquiry into the conspiracy of the murder of Gandhi was set. RSS leaders were acquitted of the conspiracy charge by Supreme Court of India. Following his release in August 1948, Golwalkar wrote to Prime Minister Jawaharlal Nehru to lift the ban on RSS. After Nehru replied that the matter was the responsibility of the home minister, Golwalkar consulted Vallabhbhai Patel regarding the same. Patel then demanded on absolute precondition that the RSS adopt a formal written constitution and make it public, where Patel expected RSS to pledge its loyalty to the Constitution of India, accept the tricolour as the national flag of India, define the power of the head of the organization, make the organization democratic by holding internal elections and acquiring the authorization of parents before enrolling their preadolescents into the movement, and renounce violence and secrecy. The RSS initially resisted the demands but later on complied with them.

On 11 July 1949, the government of India lifted the ban on the RSS by issuing a communiqué stating that the decision to lift the ban on the RSS had been taken in view of the RSS leader Golwalkar's undertaking to make the group's loyalty towards the Constitution of India and acceptance and respect of the national flag of India more explicit in the Constitution of the RSS, which was to be worked out in a democratic manner.

After India had achieved independence, the RSS was one of the sociopolitical organizations that supported and participated in movements to decolonize Dadra and Nagar Haveli, which at that time was ruled by Portugal.

The capture of Dadra and Nagar Haveli gave a boost to the movement against Portuguese colonial rule in the Indian subcontinent. In 1955 RSS leaders demanded the end of Portuguese rule in Goa and its integration into India. When Prime Minister Jawaharlal Nehru refused to provide an armed intervention, RSS leader Jagannath Rao Joshi led the satyagraha agitation straight into Goa. Goa was later annexed into the Indian Union in 1961 through an army operation, code-named Operation Vijay, which was carried out by the Nehru government.

After the declaration of 1971 Bangladesh War of Independence by Indira Gandhi, RSS provided support to the government by offering its service to maintain law and order in Delhi, and its volunteers were apparently the first to donate blood.

In 1975 the Indira Gandhi government proclaimed emergency rule in India, thereby suspending fundamental rights and curtailing the freedom of the press. This action was taken after the Supreme Court of India cancelled her election to the Indian Parliament on charge of malpractices in the election. Democratic institutions were suspended, and prominent opposition leaders, including Gandhian Jayaprakash Narayan, were arrested, while thousands of people were detained without any charges taken up against them. RSS—which was seen as being close to opposition leaders and, with its large organizational base, was seen to have the capability of organizing protests against the government—was also banned. Emergency was lifted in 1977, and as a consequence, the ban on the RSS was also lifted.

The emergency is said to have legitimized the role of RSS in Indian politics, which had not been possible ever since the stain the organization had acquired following Mahatma Gandhi's assassination in 1948, thereby 'sowing the seeds' for the Hindutva politics of the following decade. In the year 1980, the Bharatiya Janata Party was formed as a political arm of RSS. Initially, it did not do well in election, but since 1996, it has been rising and today has absolute majority in Lok Sabha and also rules a number of states.

Vishva Hindu Parishad

It was founded in 1964 by M. S. Golwalkar and S. S. Apte in collaboration with Swami Chinmayananda. Its stated objective is 'to organize, consolidate the Hindu society and to serve, protect the Hindu Dharma'. The fourteenth Dalai Lama is a member of the VHP and was present at its founding. The VHP—which considers Buddhists, Jains, and Sikhs as well as native tribal religions as part of the greater Hindu fraternity—officially mentions that it was founded by the 'Saint Shakti of Bharat'.

The VHP is a member of the Sangh Parivar group, an umbrella of Hindu nationalist organizations led by the Rashtriya Swayamsevak Sangh (RSS). It has been involved in controversial issues in India, such as construction and renovation of Hindu temples, issues of cow slaughter, religious conversion, the Ayodhya dispute, and its role in the Babri Masjid demolition.

Bajran Dal

It is an extremist and militant Hindu organization that forms the youth wing of the Vishva Hindu Parishad (VHP) and a member of the RSS family of organizations. The ideology of the organization is based on Hindutva (Hindu nationalism). Founded on 1 October 1984 in Uttar Pradesh, it has since spread throughout India, although its most significant base remains the northern and central portions of the country. The group runs about 2,500 akhadas, similar to the shakhas (branches) of the Rashtriya Swayamsevak Sangh. The name Bajrang is a reference to the Hindu deity Hanuman.

The Bajrang Dal's slogan is 'Seva Suraksa Sanskriti', or 'Service, safety, and culture'. One of the main goals of the Dal is to build the Ram Janmabhoomi temple in Ayodhya.

Akhil Bharatiya Akhara Parishad

Also called All-India Akhara Council, it is the apex organization of Hindu *sants* (saints) and sadhus (ascetics) in India. The ABAP is composed of fourteen akharas or organizations of Hindu sants and sadhus. Nirmohi Akhara (involved in the Ram Janmabhoomi dispute in Ayodhya) and Shri Dattatreya Akhara are two of the prominent akharas which are part of it. The Akhil Bharatiya Akhara Parishad is based on the system of akharas in Hindu society. An *akhara* literally means a 'wrestling ring' in Hindi, but it also stands for 'place of debate'. There are fourteen such organizations based on the form of Hinduism and Hindu philosophy they adhere to. Recently, the Akhil Bharatiya Akhara Parishad came into the limelight when it released a list of fourteen fake babas and demanded legislation against cult leaders.

International Society for Krishna Consciousness (ISKCON)

Founded in the year 1966 in the USA by A. C. Bhaktivedanta Swami Prabhupada, it has a significant presence in most of the major cities in India as well as abroad.

ISKCON was formed to spread the practice of bhakti yoga, in which those involved (bhaktis) dedicate their thoughts and actions towards pleasing the Supreme Lord Krishna. ISKCON as of 2009 is a worldwide confederation for more than 650 temples and centres, including 60 farm communities (some aiming for self-sufficiency), 50 schools, and 90 restaurants. Its most rapid expansions in membership as of 2007 have been within India and, especially after the collapse of the Soviet Union, Eastern Europe.

ISKCON advocates preaching. Members try to spread the Krishna consciousness primarily by singing the Hare Krishna mantra in public places and selling books written by Bhaktivedanta Swami. Both of these activities are known within the movement as Sankirtan. Street preaching is one of the most visible activities of the movement. ISKCON street evangelists sometimes invite members of the public to educative activities, such as a meal with an accompanying talk. Within ISKCON, women are renowned and regarded as completely equal to men in regard to spirituality.

Swaminarayan Sampraday

Known previously as the Uddhav Sampraday, this Hindu sect was propagated by Sahajanand Swami, who was born on 2 April 1781 and passed away on 1 June 1830.

Followers of the faith are called Satsangis and are expected to follow the certain basic rules set forth by Swaminarayan. Since its inception, the sect has had a huge number of ascetics who have contributed towards the growth and development of the movement and the salvation of its members. They have a special responsibility to take care of images in temples. These ascetics wear orange robes and lead a strict life, refraining from worldly pleasures and devoting their lives to the service of the fellowship. The Swaminarayan Sampraday has temples on five continents. Six temples that Swaminarayan built during his lifetime are considered to be the most important within the faith.

The Swaminarayan Sampraday has its roots in the Vedas. It follows the Vaishnava tradition and, to its followers, represents a form of Hinduism. Swaminarayan built a number of temples during his time and, except in Saharanpur, installed Krishna as central deity in each. The faith focuses on salvation through total devotion (or bhakti) to the God developed through virtues (dharma), spiritual wisdom (*gnana*), and detachment (*vairagya*).

The Swaminarayan Sampraday is focused on devotion and advocates God within the disciplines of virtues. Swaminarayan propagated a philosophy called vairagya, which says that God is supreme, has a divine form, is the all-doer, and is completely independent. He simply stated that souls (*jiva*) never merge or dissolve into God; neither are they part of God but are always subservient of God. Redemption consists in the realization of *ekantik* dharma, comprising righteousness, right knowledge, detachment, and devotion to that God.

The Swaminarayan Sampraday aims to consolidate characters in society, families, and individuals by mass motivation and individual attention through elevating projects for all, irrespective of class, creed, colour, and country. The organization believes that the hallmark of the Swaminarayan devotee is that he or she devoutly begins the days with puja and meditation, works or studies honestly, and donates regular hours in serving others. Swaminarayan's lifetime objective for the organization was to establish a permanent system of achieving the ultimate redemption from the cycle of life and death (*atyantik kalyan*).

One of the most prominent features of the heritage of Swaminarayan is its temple architecture. The images in the temples built by Swaminarayan are the evidence of the priority of Krishna. All the temples constructed during his life show some form of Krishna, and all temples since have such worshipped figures, or *murtis*.

Apart from large number of temples in India, the Swaminarayan sect has many notable temples overseas in the US, UK, Australia, Seychelles, Canada, Thailand, Fiji, Mauritius, New Zealand, Oman, UAE, and Zambia.

The expertise of Swaminarayan Sampraday members in constructing Hindu temples is going to be a big boon for the upcoming Maha Mandir.

Ramakrishna Mission

The mission is named after and inspired by the Indian saint Ramakrishna Paramahamsa and founded by Ramakrishna's chief disciple, Swami Vivekananda, on 1 May 1897. The mission—which is headquartered near Kolkata at Belur Math in Howrah, West Bengal—subscribes to the ancient Hindu philosophy of Vedanta. It aims at the harmony of religions and promoting peace and equality for all humanity.

Ramakrishna Paramahamsa (1836–1886), regarded as a nineteenth-century saint, was the inspiration of the Ramakrishna Order of monks and is regarded as the spiritual founder of the Ramakrishna Movement. Ramakrishna was a priest in the Dakshineswar Kali Temple and attracted several monastic and householder disciples. Narendranath Dutta, who later became

Vivekananda, was one of the chief monastic disciples. According to Vrajaprana, shortly before his death in 1886, Ramakrishna gave the ochre cloth to his young disciples, who were planning to become renunciates. Ramakrishna entrusted the care of these young boys to Vivekananda. After Ramakrishna's death, the young disciples of Ramakrishna gathered and practised spiritual disciplines. They took informal monastic vows on a night which, to their pleasant surprise, turned out to be the Christmas Eve in 1886.

After the death of Ramakrishna in 1886, the monastic disciples formed the first *math* (monastery) at Baranagar. Later Vivekananda became a wandering monk, and in 1893, he was a delegate at the 1893 Parliament of the World's Religions. His speech there, beginning with 'Sisters and brothers of America', became famous and brought him widespread recognition. Vivekananda went on lecture tours and held private discourses on Hinduism and spirituality. He also founded the first Vedanta Society in the United States, in New York. He returned to India in 1897 and founded the Ramakrishna Mission on 1 May 1897. Though he was a Hindu monk and was hailed as the first Hindu missionary in modern times, he exhorted his followers to be true to their faith but to respect all religions of the world, as his guru Ramakrishna had taught that all religions are pathways to God. One such example is his exhortation that one can be born in a church but he or she should not die in a church, meaning that one should realize the spiritual truths for themselves and not stop at blindly believing in doctrines taught to them.

The Ramakrishna Mission is administered by a governing body which is composed of the democratically elected trustees of Ramakrishna Math. The headquarters of Ramakrishna Math at Belur (popularly known as Belur Math) serves also as the headquarters of the Ramakrishna Mission. A branch centre of Ramakrishna Math is managed by a team of monks posted by the trustees led by a head monk with the title Adhyaksha. Ramakrishna Mission is governed by a managing committee consisting of monks and laypersons appointed by the governing body of Ramakrishna Mission, whose secretary, almost always a monk, functions as the executive head.

The principal workers of the mission are the monks. The mission's activities cover education, healthcare, cultural activities, rural uplift, tribal welfare, youth movement, etc.

The mission has its own hospitals, charitable dispensaries, maternity clinics, tuberculosis clinics, and mobile dispensaries. It also maintains training centres for nurses. Orphanages and homes for the elderly are included in the mission's field of activities, along with rural and tribal welfare work.

The mission has established many renowned educational institutions in India, having its own university, colleges, vocational training centres, high schools and primary schools, teacher training institutes, as well as schools for the visually handicapped. It has also been involved in disaster relief operations during famine, epidemic, fire, flood, earthquake, cyclone, and communal disturbances.

The mission is a non-sectarian organization and ignores caste distinctions. Ramakrishna ashram's religious activities include satsang and *arati*. Satsang includes communal prayers, songs, rituals, discourses, reading, and meditation. Arati involves the ceremonial waving of lights before the images of a deity or holy person and is performed twice in a day. Ramakrishna ashrams observe major Hindu festivals, including Maha Shivratri, Rama Navami, Krishna Ashtmi, Durga Puja. They also give special place to the birthdays of

Ramakrishna, Sarada Devi, Swami Vivekananda, and other monastic disciples of Ramakrishna. January 1 is celebrated as Kalpataru Day.

The math and the mission are known for their religious tolerance and respect for other religions. Among the earliest rules laid down by Swami Vivekananda for them was 'Due respect and reverence should be paid to all religions, all preachers, and to the deities worshipped in all religions'. Acceptance and toleration of all religions is one of the ideals of Ramakrishna Math and Mission. Along with the major Hindu festivals, Christmas Eve and Buddha's birthday are also devoutly observed.

Arya Samaj

It is an Indian Hindu reform movement that promotes values and practices based on the belief in the infallible authority of the Vedas. The *samaj* was founded by the sannyasi (ascetic) Dayananda Saraswati on 7 April 1875. Members of the Arya Samaj believe in one god and reject the worship of idols.

With the change of times, the Arya Samaj has been marginalized by the Hindu society in India. The facilities created by the old Arya Samaj are now used for Hindu marriages by the people who believe in simplicity. It hardly has any new followers.

Apart from the Swaminarayan Sampraday (which is more a Hindu sect rather than an organization) and Ramakrishna Mission, the main Hindu organization that India has today is Rashtriya Swayamsevak Sangh. It has a history of more than ninety years and has a political wing called Bharatiya Janata Party, which rules the central government as well as many states of India. The newly formed Maha Mandir shall have to deal with utmost caution and care with RSS, which has been an umbrella Hindu organization to many small outfits. The huge experience of some RSS leaders is really going to be helpful to Maha Mandir, and maybe an RSS leader can be the apex Hindu priest.

The Hindu Mythology and Festivals

$\mathcal{M}$ ost Hindus, when asked whether Mahabharata and Ramayana are mythology or a part of history, are not comfortable. Even the experts on Hindu mythology are not ready to concede that both Mahabharata and Ramayana are not part of human history. They go on expressing their views that when all the Hindus have deep faith in these two epics, we have to consider them as part of human history. Both the epics provide lots of teachings and guidance to all Hindus. Anybody who expresses that they are not part of human history faces the irritation of fellow Hindus. How could the crores of Hindus, who have been worshipping Krishna and Rama as gods for centuries, be wrong? Here lies a big challenge for the newly formed Maha Mandir.

The holy book Gita is part of the great epic Mahabharata. The Lord Krishna narrates Gita to Arjuna when he was in a dilemma whether to raise arms against his own cousins and other relatives. The Lord Krishna insisted that to defend the truth, he had to fight and raise the arms against anybody, including his relatives and dear ones. There could not be any compromise. He succeeded in convincing Arjuna and readied Arjuna for full-fledged war.

The narration by Lord Krishna is just wonderful that nobody can believe that it has actually not happened and is only a part of an epic. The Gita for Hindus is as holy as the Bible for Christians and the Quran for Muslims. The content is so rich that only a god could have narrated it. If the Hindus are forced to believe that the Mahabharata is not part of human history, the holy Gita also has to be taken as not narrated by a god. This can deeply hurt the feelings of all Hindus.

The Maha Mandir has to accept the challenge and educate all the Hindus that the Mahabharata and Ramayana are not part of history but are the greatest epics and greatest works of literature ever written by anybody on earth. The Hindus may continue to visit the temples with the idols of Lord Krishna, Rama and Sita, Laxman, Hanuman, and so on but with the clear knowledge that they are not part of human history. It is imperative for the Maha Mandir to do so.

Similarly, Lord Shiva, Parvati, Brahma, Vishnu, Ganpati, and Durga belong to the ancient form of mythology. The Hindus believe that all these gods have existed for thousands of years, even before Hinduism came into existence. Once again, no Hindu is going to believe that all these gods are not part human history— particularly the goddess Durga, who is worshipped in various forms in different states in northern India, Gujarat, and West Bengal.

Many Hindu priests continuously preach Bhagwad Gita for seven–eight days, and similarly they do so with the Ramayana. Thousands of Hindu devotees turn up to listen to them. The narration is also broadcast live on television. How are the Hindus going to believe that what the priest is narrating is just an imagined story?

Prior to the onset of winter every year, people in West Bengal offer prayers to Maa Durga and people in Gujarat worship Maa Durga by dancing the garba. Prior to the onset of summer, every year people in Punjab, Delhi, Haryana, and many other North Indian states offer prayers to Maa Durga in the form of *jagrata*. The atmosphere during all these festivals is lively and filled with devotion towards the goddess Maa Durga.

In most of northern states as well as Bihar, prior to the onset of winter, the people perform Ram Lila for nine days, finishing with Ravan Dahan on Dusshera. These days are of utter importance for all the Hindus in the northern states.

For about a century, the Maharashtrians have been celebrating Ganesha Utsava for ten days before the end the of monsoon season every year. In all these days, people meet and greet each other. The atmosphere is filled with great devotion for Lord Ganesha. The sentiments of all the Hindus are going to be hurt if they are told that Lord Ganesha never existed in human history. About two decades back, there was a chain of rumours that the idols of Lord Ganesha were sucking the milk offered by the devotees in all Ganesha temples throughout India. Millions of Hindu devotees rushed to Ganesha temples, offering milk, and the rumours spread throughout India like wildfire. This kind of incident is unparalleled in human history and was a matter of talk throughout the world in those days. It only shows the blind faith of Hindus in miracles. The miracles have taken their toll on many Hindu devotees, landing them in the grip of many false god-men.

Dealing with the mythological part of Hinduism is no doubt going to be a tough task for the Maha Mandir, but if the subject is not dealt with, lots of reforms in Hinduism cannot take place. The very important part is the water pollution of rivers throughout India as well as the seashores of Mumbai and Maharashtra.

At the end of the Ganesha festival, the devotees immerse the idols of Ganesha into the river waters, with lots of fanfare. Hundreds of devotees throughout India die while immersing the idols because of accidents. The biggest problem is water pollution because of immersing these idols. The society and politicians find themselves helpless in preventing devotees from doing so.

Formation of the Maha Mandir can immensely help to educate the people on river pollution as well as so many types of pollutions created by the religious day-to-day activities in Hinduism. Recently, since the last decade, the people of Gujarat State have also started worshipping Lord Ganesha. Scores of pandals are created in urban areas, obstructing the vehicle traffic as well as creating noise in the evening. They are even located near certain hospitals. Till now only the Marathis staying in towns and cities of Gujarat celebrated the Ganesha festival, but now people celebrate the Ganesha festival at par with the Navratri festival, which falls only after a month at the end of the Ganesha festival. Once again, the society leaders as well as political leaders just can't do anything to stop the new practice. The few people who do not have much to do as routine work gather and start collecting funds from the neighbourhood, whether in a street or a marketplace. People oblige them for fear that they might harm their interests since they are free most of the time in a day. Mania catches on, and lots of Ganesha pandals came up. These groups of free people need not give any account of money received and money spent to anybody.

The Maha Mandir can do lots of reforms in the management of festivals celebrated publicly throughout the India.

In old times, before fifty years or more, the urban population was less than 20 per cent of today's population. The vehicles were less, maybe about 10 per cent of today's vehicle population. The festivals in those days were a matter of joy for everybody since life was very slow and people had enough spare time. But life in modern days is hectic, particularly in urban areas, and there is lots of traffic on roads and market areas. The celebration of festivals sometimes creates lots of troubles to the people, and the organizers are not ready to consider the difficulties faced by the common people. Sometimes the students' exams are near, and there is a lot of noise going around. Sometimes some aged people want to sleep, but there's noise going on even after midnight. For the patients under treatment in hospitals, these sometimes create lots of problems. The Maha Mandir with teeth is the only solution to these problems.

Most of the time, the festival celebrators and the organizers cite the old traditions to justify their conduct. Particularly in Mumbai during the month of August or September, at the time of the Janmashtami festival, the celebrators of Dahi Handi go on building a human pyramid with a height of as high as fifty feet. This happens due to negative competition instigated by certain social leaders as well as the political leaders. The results are, many people lose their lives, and hundreds of people are injured. The celebrators go on citing the traditions. Nobody dares to ask them, 'Was it so one hundred years ago?' The Maha Mandir with teeth can educate the participants of the Dahi Handi festival. The human life is precious, and nobody should die or get hurt while celebrating a festival. The parents whose children are victims of this mania know better.

The Diwali festival for Hindus in India is what the Christmas is for the Christians throughout the world.

All the Hindus try to reach their parents' homes during the Diwali festival. Diwali is called the festival of lights. People decorate their houses with a series of bulbs and diyas. The festival of lights has now become more a festival of noise. Throughout India, firecrackers worth crores of rupees are cracked during the festival; most of them are imported from China. Firefighters are on high alert during the Diwali festival. Many people incur injuries, and sometimes some people even lose their eyesight due to accidents from firecrackers. There are also people who cite the old traditions, but there were no firecrackers used in India before the year 1940. Advanced countries also do not allow the use of firecrackers.

The ordinary citizens of a nation are like children. The latest trend is that the firecrackers are available throughout the year in particular shops in most of the cities, and they are used in wedding processions. The trend is fast increasing. A wedding procession is a matter of joy for the people participating in it, but it is a headache for the people around. Sometimes affected citizens call the police to stop the use of firecrackers. There is nobody to guide the people on this account; only the Maha Mandir can do it.

The latest disturbing development is the use of firearms during a wedding procession. Some drunk people fire shots in the air to show their joy. Sometime a person is killed or hurt. In old times, people from the ruling class, particularly in Rajasthan and Gujarat and wherever there were princely states, had a tradition of firing in the air to show their joy during a wedding procession. Now there are scores of people equipped with legal or illegal firearms, and accidents have increased. There is nothing to justify this kind of practice. The Maha Mandir has to stop it without any delay.

The Sankranti festival is celebrated more in Gujarat and Rajasthan during the month of January every year. People fly kites while standing on roofs of their houses and compete with others. Sometimes they use the thread with glass coating. There are even incidences of throat cutting and injuries to people. Lots of people fall down from the terraces and are injured. In addition, lots of people are injured on roads while chasing a falling kite.

The latest additional cause of fire at night is the Chinese balloon, a sort of kite called *tukkal*. The sky looks beautiful when there are hundreds of tukkals flying in the night, but some of them fall down and cause fire. The property loss is sometimes immense. The governments in recent years have banned the Chinese tukkals, but still people fly them. There are traders who illegally import these tukkals and sell them to the public without knowledge of the potential damage the tukkals can cause. The Maha Mandir can definitely stop the practice and educate people. The only solution is that people should fly the kites from the ground level not from the terraces of their homes. The level to fun will come down, but then people ought to know that kite-flying competitions are organized on ground level. The competitors are not allowed to fly their kites from terraces.

Where the social and political leaders have failed, the Maha Mandir can definitely succeed. Any modern society cannot tolerate any potential injury or death during the celebrations of all festivals. There have to be clear guidelines, and the people have to follow them. The Maha Mandir can play a leading catalyst role in this regard. Right now there is a mania of mobs ruling most of the festivals. The mobs may not have the right knowledge of any potential damage.

One major problem which has developed with the Hindu festivals in the last three decades is that now the fun is associated with worshipping in Hindu festivals in India. In all religious matters the world over, irrespective of any religion, worshipping of a god is a serious business and not fun. You cannot find fun associated with any of the Christian, Buddhist, or Muslim festivals. There is a difference between joy and fun. People express their joy during the festivals of Eid or Christmas. Recently, some of the Indian festivals have become occasions for fun for some people.

Particularly in Gujarat, the Navratri festival is now celebrated with added fun for youngsters in addition to regular worshipping of the goddess Durga for the old generation. Young boys and girls in large cities go on playing disco *dandiya* till the early morning with loud music. It's fun for them, but neighbourhoods are disturbed like anything. It is not an old tradition, but the young generation has carried on the new mania in competition with each other. The local police department takes action to restrict the disco dandiya till midnight, but the youth deny them many times and go on late into the night. The politicians encourage such a practice because it's popular.

Another example of fun during a festival is playing loud music during jagrata in the northern part of India. In these parties for the singing of devotional songs, sometimes they sing tunes based on songs from films, and sometimes the noise is too loud for the people in neighbourhood. This new practice has developed only during last two or three decades. Jagarata used to be about the matter of singing devotional songs for the goddess Durga.

The Hindu festival of Holi really belongs to fun and not for the devotion to gods or goddesses. People play with dry and water colours and apply colours on each other. People go to each other's house, sometimes in groups. The spirit of this festival has also been marred by some overenthusiastic people for the last few decades. The police department has to be on vigil so that notorious young boys don't harass girls. Some antisocial element use hard colours while playing the Holi. Sometimes it takes days to remove these colours from the skin. Many newspapers, TV channels, and local radio stations every year come up with an appeal to the people not to play with fast colours. They also appeal to minimize the use of water since there is always a shortage of running water in almost all cities of India. Still as the day passes by, people start ignoring the appeal just for their fun. The Maha Mandir can play an important role in educating the people.

There are so many Hindu festivals in India where people like to celebrate and participate in masses. Some are celebrated in devotion to gods and goddesses, and some are celebrated traditionally for joy and fun. In India, about 60 per cent of the population are people below the middle class. This population below the middle class likes to forget their day-to-day problems by widely participating in festivals.

There is one tradition of bull fights called Jallikattu, which is held in the state of Tamil Nadu during the month of January every year. The Supreme Court of India had banned the Jallikattu, but last January, the people of Tamil Nadu demanded the ban to be lifted. The political parties supported them, and the court had to budge. The tradition was restored. Many people were hurt, and some even died.

The common people are like children, but the people governing them have to be mature. The Maha Mandir can play an important role in educating people on the celebration of certain festivals. All over the world, as civil societies have matured, they see that human life is very precious and so is the health of everybody.

The Maha Mandir can issue advisories on each and every festival in India and see to it that people follow them so nobody is hurt or nobody dies. It will immensely help the government in maintaining the law and order.

Coming back to mythological part of Hinduism, the people are increasingly believing in mythology rather than treating Hindu text not as history. Even the politicians and bureaucrats are supporting the popular views of Hindu texts being history rather than mythology. In a science congress held some time ago, even some scientists emphasize that India was far ahead in scientific research during the old days. They cited some examples from Mahabharata and Ramayana. Some Indian scientists who have worked in the USA were not comfortable listening to this type of narrations. Only sometime back, a minister was comparing the satellites launched by the ISRO with weaponry possessed by Lord Rama.

The civil societies the world over change with the times in light of new discoveries and the new facts coming out because of various scientific research and new beliefs developing in society. The Hindu society also cannot stick to old traditions in the name of faith and belief. The Hindus all over India in the past, before the British came, had only two holidays in a month. One on *amavasya* and another one on the eleventh day of the brighter moon. Should we restore the old practice in the age of working five days a week? If we do so, central government employees in India shall be working twenty-eight days a month instead of twenty days as of today. Similarly, the tradition of sati would continue if we go back to old traditions, and the Dalits also would be subjected to all the hatred they were facing in the past before the independence of India.

It is imperative for the Maha Mandir to educate the Hindus on the subject of mythology versus history.

Let the Hindus continue to believe in mythology, but they must know that it is not history. The spread of television came to India in the mid 1980s. For the last three decades, the mythological TV programmes have gained tremendous popularity. TV programme producers have now moved from Ramayana and Mahabharata to programmes highlighting Shiv Puran, Shani Devta, Ganesha, Hanuman, goddess Durga, and even Santoshi Maa. All these programmes are very popular with the common masses.

One solution is to educate the people by frequently putting a clip during the broadcast of mythology-based TV programmes: 'What you are watching is not history but mythology.' This is necessary for the Maha Mandir to do in order to help the Hindus live in reality.

In India, all the Hindus live with the wrong belief that our country is like a golden sparrow in King Ashoka's time. Human history does not support it. Before the industrial revolution, all over the world, 90 per cent of the human population lived in poverty. India was no different. A modern society ought to know the facts.

The Hindus consider the rivers as sacred, like cows. In old times, the population was very low, and people could afford to throw all their ritual materials into rivers as well as dead bodies into the great Ganga. The Indian government for decades has tried hard to clean the rivers but has not succeeded. The industrial waste is much more to blame for the pollution of rivers than the ritual materials thrown into rivers.

The people are requested not to throw ritual materials into the rivers, but the request is not heeded. The government cannot be so tough with the people since it's a democratic country. Here also the Maha Mandir can play an important role.

There is the Maha Kumbh Mela organized at the sangam at Allahabad, Uttar Pradesh, every twelve years, and there are three Ardh Kumbh Melas organized at Haridwar, Nasik and Ujjain between the periods of two Kumbh Melas. For centuries, the Hindus have great faith in these Kumbh Melas, and every Hindu tries to take a holy bath in the river during the Kumbh Mela.

There is no doubt that the Uttar Pradesh government takes great care to ensure the success of Allahabad Kumbh Mela every time and so do the Mahashtrian government at the occasion of Nasik Kumbh Mela and the Madhya Pradesh government at the time of Ujjain Kumbh Mela. The Allahabad Kumbh in particular is the greatest gathering of people on one occasion. Some foreign tourists also visit it to have a feel for the Kumbh phenomenon.

The Maha Mandir has to take stock of the situation and whether the Kumbh Melas can go on or not. Apart from the pollution to the river waters, it's a huge task of human mobilization. Sometimes, people lose their precious lives because of stampedes. The Maha Mandir has to look into the matter in a long-term context. It can device methods to bring down the crowds with every Kumbh Mela passing by so pollution to the river waters is minimized. It can also impose the cow protection tax on all the people visiting the Kumbh Mela to generate funds.

Some other Hindu festivals attract lakhs of visitors every year, and crowds are increasing. About twenty-five lakhs of people are supposed to have visited Ambaji Mela this year in Gujarat in spite of swine flu threat. The traffic on highways is affected by this vast movement. The Maha Mandir has to device a method to bring down the crowds.

In light of the task of cow protection, which is supposed to be handled by the Maha Mandir, a cow protection tax seems to be a legitimate idea to bring down the crowds.

The Hindu mythology and the festivals go hand in hand, as most of the festivals are based on mythological beliefs. The Ram Lila, which is celebrated for ten days prior to Diwali, is immensely popular in the whole of northern India. The festival reflects a deep faith of the people in Ramayana. All the cities are decorated, and sometimes some streets or even roads are partially blocked for the stage performance of Ram-Lila, which takes place in the evening during those days. In all the cities and towns, a major Ram-Lila is performed in large grounds which can accommodate thousands of people. The smaller Ram-Lilaas are staged in streets to satisfy the needs of the common masses. Sometimes new Ram-Lila groups are formed because of differences among the Ram-Lila organizers.

The disturbing fact is that the Ram-Lilas in streets and on roads restrict the traffic movement immensely. In modern times, all over the world, free and speedy movement of traffic is necessary. In certain cases, the Ram-Lila also affects the routine business of shopkeepers in a particularly street. The shopkeepers cannot oppose the Ram-Lila organizers, fearing their influential power.

The Maha Mandir can look into the matter and see to it that the Ram-Lilaare permitted to be organized in a manner that regular traffic moves smoothly and shopkeepers don't lose their business.

The Ganesha Visarjan during the month of September every year in Maharashtra is a very popular event with the people. The Maharashtrian people worship Ganesha at home as well as in pandals. They take out their worshipped Ganesha idol for immersion into the water after the worshipping periods of four, six, eight, and ten days. They take them out in a sort of procession with their friends and relatives when they go for immersing the idol into the water. Sometimes these groups create a lot of noise and block the traffic. There is nobody to guide them or instruct them.

On the last day of Ganesha Visarjan, there is a holiday throughout Maharashtra, particularly in Mumbai. The processions take hours to reach their destination. Particular roads are blocked. The atmosphere during the *visarjan* processions is filled with an ocean of faith, and they are worth watching. Still the Maha Mandir needs to take stock of happenings and decide if there can be any changes to the practice.

Certain pandals in Mumbai have now developed so much popularity that there are long queues of devotees. Sometimes it takes hours for a devotee to reach the idol of Ganesha. The donation receipts amount to millions of rupees, and golden ornaments also are donated by the devotees to Ganesha. The organizers of pandals are free to spend the money received as per their wish after the festival is over. There are no complaints, and the money is spent on noble causes, like medicines to the poor as well as free meals. Once the Maha Mandir is in place, all the pandals should come under its governance. The organizers of pandals must submit the money received to the Maha Mandir after the celebrations are over. It should be at the Maha Mandir's discretion where to use the money received. In the present scenario, the money can go to cow protection since the requirement of Rs.1 lakh crores per annum is a huge amount.

There is a great sense of competition among various organizers of Ganesha pandals. If one pandal goes for a Ganesha idol with a height of ten feet, another goes for twelve feet. A situation has emerged where there are Ganesha idols with a height of more than a two-story building. They are brought by cranes and then once again loaded on vehicles by the cranes for the purpose of immersing them in water during the procession. The immersion is also done by the cranes. All this is not an old tradition. The height of Ganesha idols has increased every year due to a negative competition among the pandal organizers. Some Ganesha idols belong to certain politicians and even film actors.

Here the Maha Mandir should step in. It can restrict the height of Ganesha idols. Another important thing is that the Maha Mandir can suggest using the pictures of Ganesha rather than idols for the purpose of worshipping. In the old days, even before the independence, there were limitations in printing of large pictures. In modern times, it is possible to print pictures of any size, even in 2D or 3D images. Sometimes the pictures can be more beautiful than even the idols. Perhaps pictures may not need to be immersed into the water after the completion of the festival. Many devotees should be ready to collect the pictures of Ganesha at the end of the festival by paying huge amounts. There can even be an auction, and the money received can be used for a noble cause.

The immersion of Ganesha idols causes lots of pollution to the river waters as well as damage to the ecology of seawaters. It is time for the Maha Mandir to take a firm stand and decide and then educate the people accordingly.

The immersing of Ganesha idols into water takes a toll on many lives every year. Many devotees, in overenthusiasm, reach deep waters in order to immerse the idols and lose their precious lives. Sometimes more people lose their lives when they try to save the drowning person's life. The newspapers are full of such stories every year.

The Ganesha festival is gaining popularity with every passing year throughout India; it is no longer monopolized by Maharashtrians. It is only logical because the Lord Ganesha is a common factor for all the Hindus, but many states have other festivals of their own which follow very soon after the Ganesha festival. The Indians take pride sometimes in that India is a country of festivals and that there are festivals going on round the year throughout India, but it is not good for the economic growth of the country. There are still tens of millions of people suffering dire poverty and have not much work to do. These poor people find shelter in festivals to run away from their responsibilities or day-to-day work, which in turn affects the growth of the country's GDP.

About a century back, the communist movement could gain a momentum due to the overinvolvement of people in religious activities. The communist activists found that the religious activities were like opium for the poor people and kept them away from their regular work. Thus they discouraged the people from observing their religion.

At present, the Indian population has crossed 1.3 billion and almost 70 crores of people belong to below the middle-income group. The country just cannot allow these people to pass their time unnecessarily in additional religious activities, although some regular festivals are okay. The Maha Mandir has to step in this matter and discourage all the organizers of Ganesha festival in states other than Maharashtra. Only the Maharashtrians should be allowed to organize the Ganesha festival in any state where they live in large numbers.

The Maha Mandir has to have a strong view on the organization of all festivals in India. It has to monitor all the aspects of every festival and make sure that there are no stampedes, that people are not hurt during the celebrations, or that nobody loses his or her precious life because of overenthusiasm. It should also see to it that the crowds come down so there is better management.

It is going to be possible only by disallowing free meals on the way to the destination of the festival arranged. It also has to ban the pedestrian movement of all pilgrims on highways, which is the practice in all advanced countries. It should also educate poor people, that they are not to donate a single rupee and should make better use of their savings for the education and healthcare of their children. Still if there are large crowds on certain occasions, the Maha Mandir can impose a cow protection tax on the devotees. It is going to benefit all in the long term.

Hindu Temples and Ashrams

*T*here are tens of thousands of Hindu temples throughout India as well as abroad. The mushrooming of ashrams is a recent phenomenon in Hinduism. Prior to independence, there were few ashrams throughout India. The number of ashrams has risen a thousandfold since then.

Once Maha Mandir, the apex Hindu authority, is in place, its major task is going to be the administration of all Hindu temples as well as ashrams throughout India and the world. There are very small roadside temples, small public temples situated in private places, as well as very large temples spread over acres of land throughout India. It is going to be a very tough task for the Maha Mandir to bring all the temples into its fold. The Maha Mandir has to follow the model of churches in this regard. The Maha Mandir has to see to it that sooner or later each and every temple and ashram irrespective of its size is affiliated with it.

At present, most of the temples in India are independent and not affiliated with any other temples—though some temples belong to certain sects, like

Swaminarayan, and are associated with each other. A very popular form of Vaishnava sect of Hinduism has temples called haveli in Gujarat, Maharashtra, and northern India. Some havelis are associated with each other, but most havelis are independent.

Many Hindu sects are now divided into subsects, and they have separate temples under them. There are major temples, like Tirupati Balaji, Kashi Vishvanath, Rameshwaram, Badrinath, Kedarnath, Dwarkadhish, Somnath, Jagannath Puri, etc. Four Adi Shankaracharya temples situated at Dwarka, Rameshwaram, Badrinath, and Jagannath Puri are supposed to be the seats of head priests in four directions of India. All four Shankaracharyas are supposed to be at par with each other. Whenever the matter of an apex Hindu authority is discussed, the Shankaracharyas come to people's minds. But publicly none of Shankaracharyas enjoys the respect of a head Hindu priest, not even in the eastern, southern, western, or northern part of India. There does not seem to be any harmony between the Shankracharyas. There are even more numbers of priests claiming to be Shankracharya.

There is one huge temple at Shirdi, Maharashtra, built in memory of Sai Baba. It has a huge following and cash balance as well as tens of kilograms of gold within it. The management of Sai Baba temple has even requested the Indian government for an airport at Shirdi for the convenience of devotees. Some Hindu priests have created a controversy that the Hindus should not visit the Sai temple because Sai Baba himself was a Muslim, though he had a huge Hindu following.

Till a few years back, most of the small Hindu temples were god specific. Some belong to Shiva, some to Hanuman, some to Ganesha, some to Durga, and many others to specific Hindu gods. In order to attract the devotees of other Hindu gods, most of the small Hindu temples have idols of other Hindu gods in addition to the main idol. A Hanuman temple now has idols of Durga, Ganesh, Shiva, etc. Similarly, a Shiva temple now has the idols of Hanuman, Ganesha, and Durga. The latest phenomenon in India during the last two decades is the devotion to Shani Devta among Hindus. There were a few Shani temples spread in different parts of India. Now there are hundreds of Shani temples scattered in all Indian cities. The Sai Baba temples have also spread in most Indian cities. In some cities, you can find a Sai Baba idol with a height of twenty feet or even more. There is a liking among Hindu devotees for bigger and bigger sizes of idols of Hindu gods and goddesses. The bigger the size, the more the following—and more money.

In the absence of any central Hindu authority or any monitoring authority, the Hindu temples are mushrooming in every nook and corner of the country. Sometimes a group of three or four street-smart people would put an idol of a Hindu god on the roadside, and a Hindu devotee would start visiting and worshipping that idol. There are incidents where a monkey has died because of electric shock and a small temple would go there with the name Currentwale Hanumanji. Such a temple would also attract a good number of devotees.

The administration of Hindu temples throughout India is going to be a tough and challenging task for the Maha Mandir. The apex Hindu authority has to dig into the past of each and every temple irrespective of its size. The small temples which have come up because of the smartness of a few street money-mongers have to be razed without any delay. These temples are obstacles to traffic of vehicles in cities and towns. The Maha Mandir must educate the people that the movement of vehicle traffic in modern times is of utmost priority.

While digging into the past of a small or medium-sized Hindu temple in a street, the authorities will find lots of complaints from the people residing in the neighbourhood of such temples. Some very small temples in a street have grown bigger over a period and have acquired adjoining spaces in a legal or illegal manner. When the traffic of devotees grows, the traffic of vehicles also grows. Three to four decades back, there were very few two-wheelers or four-wheelers in the country. Now there are plenty. These small temples have no parking place inside. Both the temple authorities as well as the neighbours find themselves helpless in this regard. The Maha Mandir authorities have to see to it that any municipal land is not occupied illegally. Sometimes the municipal staff also turns a blind eye when a temple encroaches on a municipal land, the matter being a religious one. The Maha Mandir need not favour anybody. It has to see to it that the neighbourhood of a temple suffers minimum hurdles.

In case of the medium- and large-sized temples, their managers generally enjoy good clout with the civic authorities as well as the police department. In many cases, the land is leased by the local authorities or state government on a very nominal amount of lease. The temple authorities build shops facing the roadside and rent them out. The charity commissioner generally does not object to this practice. The vehicle traffic near a temple doubles or sometimes triples due to the rush of devotees as well as the customers visiting the shops rented by the temple. In modern times, the shops rented by the temples command a good amount of *pagri*. It is a term used for an illegal transfer of a rented shop. Some part of the pagri goes to the temple authorities. The Maha Mandir has to see to it that there are no rented shops in any of the temples throughout India. The occupants of shops have to be given a notice of a specific period of six months or so to find alternative business places for themselves. The Maha Mandir need not compensate the shopkeepers. The space freed can be used for parking of vehicles.

In residential localities, the municipal authorities ask for a parking space of vehicles of the owners as well as the visitors in a residential complex. In case of temples, it is not possible to accommodate all the vehicles of the visitors, but the Maha Mandir must see to it that the open spaces in a compound of a temple are not occupied by the facilities created for canteen or guesthouse purposes. The Maha Mandir has to lay down the rules on accommodation to the priest who is looking after the temple. The size of the accommodation has to be minimal.

Some large temples attract thousands of devotees every day. These temples are somewhat autonomous in their own right. These temples attract large funds and even gold through offerings. There is so much gold with them that they have to deposit it with the government under some scheme. Some temples have fixed deposits amounting to hundreds of crores. Some temples are running educational institutions, and even some of them do run hospitals.

When the Maha Mandir comes into existence, it is going to be a big challenge for it to cover all the autonomous large temples in its fold. Once again here also the Maha Mandir has to lay down certain rules and regulations. It has to dig into the past of each and every priest as well as the staff of the temple concerned and filter out any criminals found. These large temples are going to be very useful in meeting the funds required for cow protection, which is almost Rs.1 lakh crores every year. The Maha Mandir has to see to it that the common people below the middle-income group from distant places don't visit the temple frequently. It has to put signboards in all such temples, requesting the people who are not income tax payers to not donate a single rupee to the temple. They should request the common people to use the money saved for their child's education and healthcare.

The Maha Mandir should also see to it that no free meals are served to the visitors. In fact, it is none of the business of the temples to serve food to regular visitors. The temples may be allowed to serve food free of cost to the local poor people once a week with full dignity. The serving of everyday food to the visitors increases the flow of devotees to the temples, but it also creates lots of hurdles for the local civic authorities. The Maha Mandir has to educate the common masses not to undertake repeated pilgrimages to distant temples. It has to educate them that they should visit local temples only and save the money on distant travels.

It should be the endeavour of Maha Mandir to see to it that all temples are well managed and the interests of devotees are protected. The Maha Mandir, in consultation with the temples, has to decide on the percentage of contribution towards the cow protection fund from the daily receipts of temples.

India is now ageing fast. Already there are more than 11 crores people in the age group of sixty plus. The figure is supposed to be doubled by year 2030. It has been observed throughout the world that the people in their old age turn towards religion to pass their time. The medium- and large-sized temples must have the necessary spaces for the elders so they can get involved with bhajans and kirtans every day. Some temples already do so, but the Maha Mandir should see to it that all the temples offer such spaces to the elders.

The Maha Mandir has to keep track of each and every temple throughout India as well as Hindu temples abroad. The Rs.1 lakh crores required for cow protection every year is a huge task. The sum is equivalent to one-time expense on a bullet train covering a 500-kilometre route every day. The Hindu temples have to be the main contributors to the cow protection fund, so the Maha Mandir must monitor the workings of each and every temple. It has to see to it that the money donated by the devotees is not wasted and all the spare funds are transferred to the cow protection fund.

Many Hindu temples have fixed deposits in banks, amounting to hundreds of crores. The Maha Mandir should see to it that the funds can be transferred to the cow protection fund. There is gold lying within the temples, valued at hundreds of crores. Some of the gold has to be utilized in the construction of the Maha Mandir itself.

As discussed earlier, the Maha Mandir must discourage the devotees with lesser income than the middle-income groups from donating. Such devotees should be educated to use the money on education and healthcare of their children. Most of the temples offer free food to the devotees to attract more and more devotees. The Maha Mandir must ask them to stop the practice; instead the temples should offer free food to local poor people once a week.

The effort by Maha Mandir is going to have additional space in many of the medium and large temples. Another good use of these spaces can be to arrange simple Hindu weddings. Many Arya Mandirs spread all over India offer these services. No Hindu temples should have night stay accommodation for the devotees; the management of temples have been offering these services to increase their influence over devotees.

The Maha Mandir must advise the central government as well as the state government not to allow any padyatra on national highways as well as state highways. It will curtail the unnecessary traffic to the temples and help to smoothen the regular traffic of vehicles. The Maha Mandir should also see to it that the charity groups don't serve free food to the pilgrims on the way to the temple. Instead they should directly remit the money to the cow protection fund. Every year, a number of people lose their precious lives in stampedes on particular occasions held in certain temples. The Maha Mandir should have a separate cell with the task of monitoring the movement of pilgrims.

Any new Hindu temple that is to be built anywhere in India must have permission from the Maha Mandir. The Maha Mandir authorities must see to it that land is legally acquired and construction is as per local civic laws. There should be enough parking spaces for two-wheelers as well as four-wheelers. The neighbourhood of any temple should have no reason to complain. The Maha Mandir should lodge a complaint with the local civic authorities to demolish the construction if a new temple comes up without prior permission from Maha Mandir.

The spread of ashrams throughout India is a new phenomenon that happened after the independence during the last seven decades. In most cases, certain gurus or god-men have been allotted the land free of cost by the state government because of their influence on the politicians. This was not possible before the independence. Some ashrams are spread beyond 100 acres of land. The value of land of certain ashrams has now reached staggering hundreds of crores because when they were built, they were in the outskirts of a city and because of the spread of urban areas, they now are very much a part of the city.

To cover all the ashrams throughout India is going to be a huge task for the Maha Mandir. Most of the gurus and god-men who happened to be in possession of ashrams have political clout. They may not like an authority looking after them and may create hurdles for the Maha Mandir. Religions like Christianity or Islam do not have any sort of ashrams; only Hinduism has them.

Recently, during the last two decades, there are complaints from followers of certain ashrams that the guru or the god-man looking after the ashram has indulged in sexual act with a devotee. The cases have gone into courts, and few god-men have been convicted after a long legal battle. Recently, the all-India Akhara Parishad has issued a list of fake god-men.

Whenever there are complaints against god-men or gurus, the politicians who are regular visitors to their ashrams blame the devotees that they should have taken care. It is the duty of the Maha Mandir, when it is in place as the highest authority of Hinduism, to serve the interests of all Hindu devotees. So it is essential that, along with all Hindu temples, all the ashrams spread throughout India are under Maha Mandir.

There are hundreds of Dera ashrams in the states of Haryana and Punjab. Many priests heading the Dera ashrams belong to the Sikh community, but they are not affiliated with any Sikh religion authority. Those Dera ashrams, who have more than 50 percent of Hindu followers and are not affiliated with any Sikh religious organization, should come under the umbrella of Maha Mandir. It is necessary to protect the interests of Hindu devotees. It is possible that some Dera ashram god-men may run to get affiliation with a certain Sikh religious organization so they are not covered by the Maha Mandir. If there are complaints from the common people about any misconduct by a Dera ashram's guru affiliated to the Sikh religion, the Maha Mandir can issue an advisory to all Hindu devotees not to visit such Dera ashram so their interests are protected.

There are hundreds of Member of Parliament, Member of Legislature Assemblies, and local civic body members with legal court cases going on against them. The cases can go on for years, sometimes for decades. They take refuge in the natural law that anybody is innocent till he or she is convicted by the law. Recently, there is a suggestion from the Supreme Court of India that the cases against such public servants should be fast-tracked so the criminal persons don't go on working in their capacity as elected representatives of the people. The gurus and god-men against whom any court cases are going on also should be covered by the fast-track courts so their devotees are safe. The Maha Mandir must develop a mechanism to inform the Hindu devotees about a court case going on against a particular god-man or guru. It should be mandatory for an ashram to put the matter in a notice for all the visitors if a court case is going on. It will compel a god-man or a guru to hasten the case going on against him if he is not at fault. The following of a guru or god-man is definitely going to be hurt till he is acquitted by the court of law. This practice is very much needed to protect the interest of the devotees, which is the prime responsibility of the Maha Mandir.

As mentioned earlier also, the Maha Mandir should dig into the past of all the gurus and god-men as well as their staff members. If there are persons with any criminal record, the Maha Mandir should get them executed in a court of law. The Maha Mandir has to go deep into the history of each and every ashram, right from the allocation of land. It should see to it that there is no illegal encroachment of land by an ashram. Many gurus and god-men have tremendous influential power in the form of their committed devotees, and they do encroachment of the adjoining land. The politicians and related authorities sometime don't object to this encroachment of land due to their good relations with the guru or god-man. The Maha Mandir should not show any mercy in this regard. In fact, it should develop a mechanism to listen to the complaints of the people staying in neighbourhood of an ashram.

The Maha Mandir has to lay down rules and regulations for the conduct of an ashram.

Generally, it is observed that the Hindu community has a great quest for miracles in their day-to-day life, and because of that quest, they seek closeness with a guru or a god-man. They are under the impression that the guru or the god-man will perform some miracle and relieve them of their pains or help them in their business or to get a better life. Many of the god-men are successful in creating the impression of a guru the devotees are looking for.

The politicians and rich businessmen join the followers of such a guru. The following takes a leap forward, and the guru achieves a pan-India appeal. He applies for land for more ashrams in other cities and gets land allotted because of his contacts with the politicians. Success brings further success. The interesting thing is that even if a devotee is cheated by the guru, he does not tell others in fear that he will be treated as a fool by the society. In some cases, the guru or god-man becomes so powerful that he is able to threaten a devotee of dire consequences if he complains about him. By that time, the guru or god-man has developed a close circle of beneficiaries who are ready to follow his commands. Some devotees who have been victimized have dared to lodge complaints against certain gurus in the recent past. Justice has taken a long time, but some gurus have been convicted.

Now comes the role of the Maha Mandir. Till now there has been no apex authority in Hinduism. The gurus or god-men should be treated as service providers by the Maha Mandir. The devotees should be treated as consumers. The Maha Mandir must protect the interests of all the devotees who visit any Hindu religious place, whether a temple or an ashram. As proposed earlier, the Maha Mandir must dig into the past of each and every guru or god-man and their staff serving him and his followers. The role of the Maha Mandir does not stop there. It has to continuously monitor each and every activity of an ashram.

A major weakness of all Indians, including the Hindus, is that they are fascinated by the talks of people. They rate a person by his talk and not by his deeds. If a person is a good orator, chances of his success are much more in public life than anybody else. It is true in the case of politicians as well as gurus, god-men, and con men. No wonder many people take advantage of this kind of weakness of Indians.

When the Maha Mandir is established as the apex authority of Hinduism, the wrong people entering as guru or god-men or even temple priests shall not succeed. Till now many gurus, god-men, and priests have self-proclaimed the titles of saint, baba, guru, *maha* guru, *sad* guru, and so on. It is imperative that the Maha Mandir must decide on certain criteria for the conferment of any title like saint, baba, guru, etc. The Maha Mandir should make it public when a person is conferred a title of baba, guru, etc. The Maha Mandir must educate all the Hindus that they should not entertain religiously unless a title is conferred by the apex authority. This kind of practice is already in demand from the public, but people are helpless in the absence of an apex Hindu authority.

Coming back to the workings of ashrams. Perhaps if accounted, the ashrams throughout India possess more land than the temples put together. The Maha Mandir has to go deep into the matter of the spread of ashrams.

In most cases, the land has been allotted by the state government free of cost or with a very nominal lease amount. The Maha Mandir authorities must assess whether a certain ashram needs the quantum of land it has. The main objective of any ashram could be to spread the thinking of a guru or god-man in the form of sermons. A guru does not need an auditorium to house an audience in excess of thousands of persons. Presently, many ashrams have accommodation facilities for the devotees as well as the staff serving the main guru. Most of the ashrams have flourished throughout India due to the absence of an apex authority of Hinduism. The Maha Mandir should show no mercy to the ashrams who have mushroomed unnecessarily. The Maha Mandir can recommend a state government to reacquire the land allotted to an ashram in toto or in part.

When the Maha Mandir is in place, it is going to be the duty of the state government to seek a recommendation by the Maha Mandir if there is any request for the building of a temple. Perhaps the society does not need the ashrams any more, but the temples are needed in new, developing housing societies or colonies. The Maha Mandir must take into account that the people residing in the neighbourhood of a temple are not disturbed. There has to be enough parking place.

The noise pollution is a recent issue troubling the people residing in the neighbourhood. In India the people compete with each other to create more noise to show that they are better devotees to their god than others. The politicians hardly take the matter seriously, and the police staff finds itself helpless to take action against anybody because of the religious activity. The noise could be from a temple or a masjid or any worshipping place.

The Maha Mandir is going to be of tremendous use in the matter of noise pollution. In most cases, the devotees put forward the argument of it being a tradition. The electronic sound system was invented only about eight decades back; it did not exist before 1930. Till then people used to worship the god with the same enthusiasm without any sound system. The Maha Mandir must enforce low levels of noise pollution depending on the location of a temple or ashram. The Maha Mandir should also issue the guidelines on sound pollution in case of any religious function to the police department. The police department must follow the instructions.

The Maha Mandir must educate the people on the subject of noise pollution. The students staying in neighbourhood of a temple or an ongoing religious function are affected by the noise in their studies. There are patients in the neighbourhood of temples who can't bear the high-decibel noise. Sometimes there are hospitals in the neighbourhood of a temple or an ongoing festival programme at a particular place. At present, the police department is helpless before religious people and don't object to the playing of loud speakers. The Maha Mandir must see to it that unnecessary high volumes of religious devotional songs are not played on speakers.

The Muslim community has formed a tradition of narrating azan on a public address system from their masjids many times a day. The narration of the azan from masjids has been taking place many times a day even before the invention of the public address system. Before the arrival of the industrial revolution and the invention of electricity, there were no machines operating here and there as well as any kind of electronic sound systems playing. There were few noises in the atmosphere, and thus, it was very calm all the time. The azan could reach distances without any sound system. The use of the sound system started around the 1940s, about seventy years back. Now there is increasing awareness about the noise pollution, so all the religious authorities, whether Hindu or Muslim, have to abide by the new rules.

Before objecting the use of the sound system by the Muslims, the Hindus also must stop creating noises. The Maha Mandir has to take suitable action in this regard.

Monkeys and Stray Dogs: A Tough Task for the Maha Mandir

*A*t last count, there were 50 million monkeys in India. The population must have risen since then.

The monkeys in India are increasingly becoming a great nuisance to the locals residing in urban areas all over India, particularly in the entire northern India and states adjoining northern India. Any person who spends five minutes in Delhi will probably meet a monkey hanging above the entrance to a nicotine shop, attempting to insert his head up its own anus. It is an amusing sight for the tourists.

The monkey population of 50 million in India is near to the entire population of United Kingdom. The situation is worsening day by day. These monkeys steal people's food and attack locals. They spread diseases and occupy houses. There were reports that in Shimla City alone, about four hundred incidences of people bitten by monkeys. The people in North Indian cities are generally vigilant while passing through the streets so that they do not encounter a monkey or that a monkey does not steal a bag from them or sometimes even their glasses. The president of India recently was advised not to wear glasses while he was visiting a particular place to avoid having it snatched by monkeys.

During the year 2007, the deputy mayor of Delhi was allegedly pushed to death from a balcony by monkeys, and there have been reports that the monkey damaged the brickwork of Chittorgarh Fort. The monkeys are also suspected to be the culprits for the missing of 11,000 official files from the Hone ministry in mysterious circumstances.

Monkeys are protected under the Wildlife Protection Act of 1972. Capturing, hunting, or killing them is a violation of the act, which may lead the offender to a judicial trial with fine, imprisonment, or both. They are considered sacred by the Hindu religion in connection with Lord Hanuman, which is a whole different breed of monkeys. 'He is a superhero of Indian god stories, and people often pay tribute to him by feeding monkeys.' During expansion in the pilgrimage site of Vridavan, Uttar Pradesh, all the way back in 1977, 600 monkeys were moved to a forest nearby, only to come wandering back a week later, more violent than before.

A 2007 high court order made it mandatory for monkeys in sanctuaries to be fed by humans rather than planting *bansa*, *gram*, and banana plants that yield fruit the monkeys can collect themselves. During the year 2013, the Indian government reportedly spent more than Rs.30 million on feeding 16,000 monkeys at the Asola Bhatti Wildlife Sanctuary. The amount spent on monkeys on average is more than the amount spent by the government on average on the human population. It is reported that the government's Forest Department spends most of its cash on feeding monkeys.

During a recent visit by Barack Obama, men were hired to chase monkeys from his path with slingshots and broomsticks. Last year, the news swept the world that men were being hired to wear large monkey costumes and squeal like langurs to chase off hordes of rhesus monkeys.

The Maha Mandir, once formed, has a great problem in the form of monkeys to deal with. The cow protection may cost a whopping Rs.1.35 lakh crores every year, but somehow it can be managed. But to find out a solution to the monkey problem in India is not going to be easy for the Maha Mandir.

The Maha Mandir has to discuss the matter with all the Hindu organizations as well as wildlife welfare groups to find some solution. The Maha Mandir should also study the practice of other countries facing monkey problems. The problem in India is entirely different because of the monkey's connection to Lord Hanuman. The religious Hindus worship cows like their mother, and the monkeys resemble their beloved god Hanuman, so they may not tolerate any harm done to the monkeys.

The Problem of Stray Dogs

India has been blaming Pakistan for the terrorist activities for the last thirty years, but the irony is that stray dogs have killed more people in India than terrorist attacks during the same period.

The population of stray dogs in India is estimated to be around 30 million as of today. As per some estimates, more than 20,000 people die of rabies every year. A couple of years back, Global Alliance for Rabies Control reported that India accounted for 35 per cent of human death from rabies, more than any other country. Many of these deaths are blamed on strays. Some time back, the high court in Kerala ordered the government to pay Rs.40,000 to a man whose wife died after contracting rabies from a dog bite. The Kerala State has reported to have more than 3,50,000 stray dogs responsible for biting more than 11,000 people who contracted rabies during the year 2015.

The health officials in Kashmir have reported that more than 50,000 locals have been bitten by feral stray dogs during the period of 2008 to 2012. A dozen people have died of rabies during that period. Similar patterns have been reported from other states throughout India. The problem with stray dogs has reached alarming levels.

The men–animal conflict is on the rise. Animal rights groups say that the cash-strapped municipalities and irate citizens have been poisoning, clubbing, beating, shooting, and electrocuting strays to control their population. Some time back, the growing stray-dog problem in Kerala and neighbouring Tamil Nadu states inspired extreme measures. Village councils ordered the killing of mutts; dog catchers hired by locals went around and injected the canines with potassium cyanide. In 2012, a lawmaker from Punjab kicked up a storm when he suggested that stray dogs should be sent to China and India's north-east, where dogs were sometimes eaten, after a rising number of dog bite cases. A parliament committee is actually 'studying in detail the management of dogs' in areas where MPs live in Delhi.

Killing of dogs has been outlawed in India since 2001. Still during the year 2008, the Mumbai High Court allowed municipal authorities to kill dogs that were creating nuisance. The Supreme Court later suspended the order. Since then as per the court order, the culling of stray dogs has been stopped; instead the court has ordered for mass dog sterilization programmes.

The number of stray dogs worldwide has been estimated between 200 and 600 million. Europe alone is estimated to have 100 million stray dogs. As per the study by the Atlanta Humane Society, there are at least five times more homeless animals than homeless people.

When certain stray dogs bite humans, they infect those people with rabies, a viral disease that causes acute inflammation of the brain. Each year, more than 15 million people are treated with post-bite rabies vaccination, while 55,000 people die of rabies; 95 per cent of rabies cases occur in Asia and Africa, and 99 per cent of rabies transmissions to humans are caused by dogs.

This situation is especially pronounced in India. The population of 30 million stray dogs amounts to 1 stray dog per 42 people in the country. By some estimates, there are more stray dogs in India than in any other country.

Delhi alone has between 2,60,000 and 4,00,000 stray dogs. According to government hospital records, there have been 77,294 dog bites in Delhi just between January and October 2015. That's a bite every 6 minutes.

An estimated 20,000 people die each year from rabies infections in India, accounting for 36 per cent of deaths from rabies worldwide. No other country has more deaths from rabies annually.

There are many reasons behind the stray dogs being so common in India.

There is a common characteristic among India's cities that encourage stray-dog populations—open garbage. Stray dogs are scavengers, so they rely on garbage on the street as a source of food. In countries where garbage is kept in bins and cleaned regularly, stray dogs cannot survive on the streets.

In many countries, the government spays and neuters stray dogs to slow population growth. Many other countries have organizations like Animal Control, the Humane Society, the SPCA, private shelters, and rescue organizations. Lately, some NGOs in India have contributed to the birth control of stray dogs.

The Maha Mandir has a tough task in its hands related to the problem of stray dogs in India. The stray dogs can't be killed or sent to China or North-East India. The Maha Mandir has to play a catalyst role to deal with problem. It has to prevail over the government as well as the Indian population to tackle the problem. It has to see that the government does well with the sterilization programmes. It has to educate the Indian public also not to feed the street dogs. It may look cruel, but that is the only remedy. It also has to educate the Indian public to see to it that the garbage in the streets is not kept open. It will discourage the survival of dogs on the streets.

The Overseas Hindus

When the census takes place in the year 2021, the total population of India is likely to reach around 138–140 crores. The Hindu population by then may cross 1.1 billion.

The population of Hindus abroad stands today in excess of 11 million. The highest density of migrant Hindus is in countries like United States, United Kingdom, Canada, New Zealand, United Arab Emirates, Saudi Arabia, and the African countries. There are millions of Hindus staying in Nepal, Pakistan, Bangladesh, Mauritius, Fiji, Indonesia, the Caribbean, and many African countries as age-old inhabitants and are contributing well to their respective economies.

The Indians overall, including Muslims, are supposed to be the most number of people living abroad as migrants. There are more numbers of Indians put together in all the countries than Chinese migrants.

The Hindus overseas have done well in creating thousands of temples to worship the Hindu gods and have created a particular identity in their new chosen land. There are hundreds of Hindu temples in Australia,

Canada, Netherlands, New Zealand, United Kingdom, and the United States of America. Some of them are famous for their decent and attractive structures, attracting thousands of devotees every day. In countries like Pakistan, Bangladesh, Nepal, Fiji, Mauritius, Indonesia, Thailand, etc. where the Hindu families have been staying for generations, there ought to be hundreds of temples.

The Swaminarayan sect of Hinduism has mastered the art of creating state-of-the-art temples around the world. Some of the Swaminarayan temples are part of tourist circuits in the United States, United Kingdom, Canada, and some other developed countries. In a latest development, a fifty-year-old church in Bear, Delaware, in the US has been converted into a Swaminarayan Hindu temple. It is the fifth church overseas to be turned into a Swaminarayan temple by Swaminarayan Gadi Sansthan based in Maninagar, Ahmedabad.

Apart from Delaware, churches in California and Kentucky in the US have been transformed into temples by the sect. Similarly, two churches have been turned into temples in London and Bolton near Manchester in the UK. The sect has also acquired a few other properties in the US, the UK, and Canada.

These temples help Hindus living in developed countries to keep the Indian culture and spirituality alive in the foreign land. The temples are open for all without preference and prejudice. The temples, apart from fulfilling religious purposes, are used to promote cultural activities, including art, drama, and craft.

The Maha Mandir shall have to create a separate cell to look after and govern all the Hindu temples out of India. The revenues of Hindu temples abroad may not be so high. The Maha Mandir cannot expect to receive much revenue from the Hindu temples abroad. On the contrary, the overseas Hindus may request for monetary help from the Maha Mandir in creating new Hindu temples. The Maha Mandir shall be obliged to do so in certain cases, but at the same time, it must see to it that huge temples are not created with a high amount for construction where the Hindu population is not so large. The Maha Mandir can request the Hindus there to divert their donations directly to the cow protection fund.

The Indians living abroad, irrespective of their religion, are the source of huge remittances to the Indian foreign exchequer, which is even higher than the remittance received by the Chinese government. The Maha Mandir can request all the Hindus abroad to donate generously and separately to the cause of cow protection in India.

The Maha Mandir, once created, is going to be a place of pilgrimage for all the Hindus staying abroad.

The So-Called Spiritual Gurus and God-Men: A Challenge for the Maha Mandir

Recently, during last few years, some Hindu spiritual gurus and god-men have been the subject of discussion and talk in the media as well as the whole society.

Prior to independence, very few gurus were known in Hindu society. It may be so because of the lack of spread through electronic media during those times and the print media also had a limited reach because of the lack of literacy among the Indian population. After the independence, the number of spiritual gurus and god-men have mushroomed all over India mainly because of patronage by the political class. The land is a state subject in India, and the gurus or god-men could prosper only because of free allotment of land by the state governments and because of the influence of certain politicians.

The situation in India has now reached a level where if the total land allotted to gurus and god-men is counted, it may turn out to be more than the total land occupied by all the Hindu temples in India. This is a worrisome matter. One may imagine that if there were no so-called gurus and god-men throughout India, how would it impact the social life? One may reply that the impact would be nil. The Maha Mandir has to look into this matter. It may be so that some spiritual gurus might have impacted the lives of certain devotees positively, but then many gurus and god-men have ruined the lives of a number of devotees. Only a few examples of spiritual god-men taking disadvantage of the blind faith of their devotees have come to light. There may be hundreds of such cases.

It is going to be the prime duty of the Maha Mandir to protect the interests of all Hindu devotees. It has to see to it that no Hindu devotee is cheated or misguided by any of the so-called spiritual guru or a god-man.

The Dera Sacha Sauda chief, Gurmeet Ram Rahim, is the latest example of a devotee being cheated by a mischievous god-man. He has been convicted of two rape cases and is now in jail. Anybody will wonder how he gained so much popularity and following. He had his *dera* spread over more than six hundred acres, more than the area of land the Christian Vatican is situated today. He also occupies many more dera ashrams in Haryana and Punjab and elsewhere.

Any civil construction going on anywhere in any city or town in India is supposed to attract the attention of local civic authorities. The civic authorities are supposed to go into the matter, whether the plans have been passed or not by their respective departments. It was found during the inspection and the search carried out by the state authorities after the arrest of the dera guru that no permissions have been obtained for the guru's properties. Anybody will wonder how such a person happened to possess so much land.

The politicians who have aided the guru to rise to such a height go on emphasizing that it is the public who blindly follows such a guru. There is no state mechanism to look into the matter, how a guru or god-man is growing so fast in the public's eye. On the contrary, such people are patronized by politicians. The Indian mentality is that whenever there are negative things about a cheater guru, the devotees not only run away but also shy away from the fact that they used to be the devotees of such a person.

There have been many more gurus and god-men who have become famous for their acts and following. The *DNA* newspaper of 17 September 2017 published some interesting facts about certain god-men and god-women of the past and present.

Late Indira Gandhi's yoga guru, Dhirendra Brahmachari, was one who ran ashrams in Delhi and Jammu and Kashmir. He became politically influential after the emergency. K. L. Shrimali lost his job as education minister after he demanded an audit report of Brahmachari's ashrams. Brahmachari, a native of Bihar, was also a source of discord between Indira and then Jammu and Kashmir chief minister Sheikh Abdullah in the late 1980s. The Jammu and Kashmir government had filed several cases against Brahmachari's gun factory. His fate declined after Indira's death in 1984.

Brahmachari's death allowed Chandraswami to emerge as a guide to politicians. He became famous for his closeness to former prime minister Narasimha Rao and wielded influence with the heads of state. Natwar Singh recalls that when he was deputy high commissioner in London in 1975, a cabinet minister wanted him to arrange a meeting between Margaret Thatcher and Chandraswami. After much pestering, he agreed to arrange a party to invite both to his residence. But Chandraswami's fall was as abrupt. In 1996, he was jailed on charges of defrauding a London-based businessman. During the year 2016, he had an obscure death.

Nirmaljit Singh Narula, alias Nirmal Baba, did not succeed as a businessman in Jharkhand. He drew publicity with his durbars and gatherings telecast by TV channels. At these events, he gave bizarre solutions to people's problems. He faced allegations of fraudulent activities. In February 2014, he was slapped with a Rs.3.5 crores service tax evasion charge. The Allahabad High Court had directed the Ministry of Information and Broadcasting in May to look into allegations that his TV programmes were spreading superstition and take action against erring channels if the charges are found to be true.

When the police arrested Sant Rampal after a two-week stand-off in Haryana's Hisar in 2014, violence spread, and six people were killed. Rampal worked as junior engineer with Haryana's irrigation department. In 1996, he resigned and set up Satlok Ashram three years later. Soon, he had a number of followers, and he opened ashrams all over Haryana. He owns a fleet of luxury cars and lives in an ashram in Barwala, Haryana, which is spread over a sprawling twelve acres.

Self-styled as a god-woman, Sukhwinder Kaur (alias Radhe Maa) likes the colour red and carries a mini *trishul*. In 2015, the Mumbai police declared her an absconder in an alleged case of dowry harassment and issued a lookout notice against her. Dolly Bindra, an actress, also filed a criminal case against her. The Punjab and Haryana High Court on 5 September issued a notice against the Kapurthala SSP for failing to act on a complaint against her. Phagwara-based Surinder Mittal had lodged a complaint against her, seeking action for allegedly hurting religious sentiments.

Asaram Bapu is one of the most controversial self-styled god-men in India. He was accused of sexually abusing a sixteen-year-old girl at his Jodhpur ashram even as her mother was waiting outside. He has been in prison on rape charges since 2013. He is also facing allegations of murder and land-grabbing. Asaram and his son were also investigated for the mysterious deaths of two boys whose decomposed bodies were found on the banks of the Sabarmati River near his ashram in 2008. The Asaram Bapu trusts have a turnover of Rs.350 crores. He owns 350 ashrams in the country and abroad. He also owns 17,000 Bal Sanskar Kendras.

The Akhil Bharatiya Akhara Parishad, the apex body of sadhus, recently released a list of fourteen 'fake babas' and demanded a crackdown on 'rootless cult leaders' by bringing in legislation. The list includes the names of Asaram Bapu (Asumal Sirumalani), Sukhbinder Kaur (Radhe Maa), Sachhidanand Giri (Sachin Datta), Gurmeet Singh of Dera Sacha Sauda, Om Baba (Vivekanand Jha), Nirmal Baba (Nirmaljit Singh), Ichchadhari Bhimanand (Shivmurti Dwivedi), Swami Asimanad, Om Namah Shivay Baba, Narayan Sai, Rampal, Acharya Kushmuni, Brahaspati Giri, and Malkhan Singh. Parishad president Swami Narendra Giri said, 'We appeal to the common people to beware of such charlatans who belong to no tradition and, by their questionable acts, bring disrepute to sadhus and sanyasis.'

The proposed apex Hindu religious body, the Maha Mandir, is going to be a big boon for all the Hindu devotees. After the incident of Dera Sacha Sauda chief Gurmeet Ram Rahim Singh's arrest, there are demands from the public that there has to be an authority to grant the titles of saint, baba, guru, maha guru, bapu swami, sadhwi, guru *maa*, etc. to certain self-proclaiming spiritual gurus and god-men. As discussed elsewhere in this book, the Maha Mandir should treat the devotees as consumers of services or sermons delivered by gurus and god-men—the service providers.

The Maha Mandir must develop a certain mechanism to ensure that no fake babas enter the fray. Any person who wants to claim himself or herself as a spiritual person along with a title of baba, guru, etc. must approach the Maha Mandir first. The Maha Mandir should have certain criteria for judging a person as a spiritual teacher. Only a person who passes through the criteria set by the Maha Mandir should be allowed to teach spirituality to the public. The Maha Mandir can also reserve certain titles for different categories of teachers depending upon their abilities and knowledge. The title can be upgraded by the Maha Mandir if asked for by the spiritual teacher.

The Maha Mandir should also stop any new allotment of land by the state governments to any spiritual teacher without its prior permission. The land allotted to present spiritual teachers is already much more in excess than needed. The Maha Mandir should carry out a scrutiny and either surrender the excess land to the government or acquire it for the purpose of construction of a new temple or cow shelters or even for certain religious activities deemed fit by it.

The spirituality is a core matter of Hinduism, and any activity related to it must be governed by the Maha Mandir. The Maha Mandir should see to it and regularly monitor it also that the spiritual teachers don't lead a luxurious life. The income generated by the teaching of spirituality has to go to the common Hindu masses, and no teacher should have a right to pocket it. Once the Maha Mandir monitors the spiritual teachings thoroughly, the fake gurus shall not dare to enter to the field of spirituality.

The teaching of yoga also falls in the category of spirituality, and its a monopoly of the Hinduism. The yoga gurus should be treated at par with other spiritual teachers. The practice of yoga has to be carried out under the supervision of an experienced yoga teacher. All the yoga teachers should have necessary permission from the Maha Mandir before they start doing so. The yoga teachers may teach yoga privately from the home or in any institution, school, college, or any ashram. One must have the permission from the Maha Mandir. There are reports that yoga, if done wrongly, damages the body. The Maha Mandir must guide and educate the people on the subject of yoga that they must learn it from the teachers certified by the Maha Mandir. It is needless to say that yoga teachers, along with spiritual teachers, should not be allowed to pocket huge incomes.

As discussed in the chapter related to cow protection, the Maha Mandir needs Rs.1 lakh crores every year to shelter and feed about 1,80,000,00 cows. All the branches of Hinduism—namely, spirituality, yoga, Ayurveda, astrology, and Vastu Shastra—have to contribute to the kitty of the Maha Mandir to meet the expenses for cow protection.

Some spiritual gurus have grown very tall during the last two to three decades and have become famous throughout the world for their teachings of spirituality as well as yoga. Few of them have also ventured into Ayurveda. The Maha Mandir, being a new identity, may find itself small before these spiritual gurus, who are very tall in their status. The Maha Mandir must perform its duty well.

The Maha Mandir should regularly collect a certain percentage from the income of all the ashrams.

Direct Cash Subsidies into the Bank Accounts of the Poor

*A*s discussed in earlier chapters, the main purpose behind the creation of the Maha Mandir, the apex governing body of Hinduism, is to abolish the caste system entirely from Hinduism.

As of today, the scheduled castes and scheduled tribes in addition to certain backward castes enjoy the benefit of reservation in education, government jobs, and political constituencies. Once the caste system is abolished by the Maha Mandir, all the benefits will go. Once there is no caste system, there is no question of any benefit based on anybody's caste, but as discussed earlier, it is likely to create a sort of chaos.

The reservation benefits are designed currently to help the poor families from Dalits, scheduled tribes, and some backward castes. The people from these communities pass their life with the illusion that one day a person from their family will get the benefit of reservation. The facts remain that only one out of twenty, or say 5 per cent, are successful in reaping the reservation benefits. The benefit they derive is as at

110

great cost of self-esteem, labelling them as persons from lower Hindu castes.

Where only one out of twenty people from the lower-caste Hindu strata has been reaping the reservation benefits, a direct cash subsidy into the bank accounts of the poor is going to benefit all people irrespective of caste and religion. There is already a demand going on for reservations in government jobs for the poor from higher Hindu castes.

Let us understand the direct cash transfers into the bank accounts of the poor. It has been the practice in most developing countries for decades. It is nothing but a 'Robin Hood approach' by governments. The governments collect revenues in the form of taxes from rich people and transfer a part of it to the bank accounts of the poor. This direct cash transfer scheme stops the leakages of money to undeserving people. At present, the Indian government spends lakhs and crores of rupees as subsidy in the distribution of grains and other items of general consumption at low or very low prices. Since the bulk of poor families have very little purchasing power, a good percentage of commodities are diverted to undeserving groups.

India already has crores of Jan Dhan accounts in the name of poor families initiated by Prime Minister Modi, so it is not going take much time in switching over to a direct cash subsidy transfer scheme.

How Does the Scheme Work?

If a family of five persons consumes twenty kilograms of wheat every month and they are made to pay Rs.15 more per kilogram to buy from the open market, they are entitled to receive Rs.300 every month as part of the direct subsidy into their bank account. Similarly, there are so many items that are going to cost more when there are no ration shops. A gas cylinder may cost more once the subsidies are withdrawn. A poor family deserves to be paid the difference in amount every month.

Once the direct cash subsidy transfer scheme is in place, ration shops or the warehouses of the Food Corporation will not be necessary. Then the government of India does not need to procure grains at minimum support price from the farmers. The farmers shall be selling their produce directly in the market at higher prices, and the difference is going to be paid to the consumers by the government in the form of a direct cash transfer.

The direct cash transfer is also going to take care of money spent by the poor families on their healthcare as well as their insurance premiums. At present, there are 15 crores families in India, estimated to be in the groups of poor, very poor, and lower middle class. The GDP of India now stands in excess of 150 lakh crores, and taxes collected by the central government as well as state governments are in excess of 25 lakh crores.

There is no reason why the Indian government shall not be able to spare 15 per cent of its revenue for direct cash transfer scheme in lieu of subsidized distribution of grain and other commodities for general consumption.

As discussed earlier, the eradication of the caste system may pose a challenge to the leadership of Dalits in the country. They may claim that the Dalits have not come out of poverty in general during the seventy years of independence and need a more level playing field in the form of reservation benefits. A solution to their demand is that the Dalit families should be paid 50 per cent more amount in their bank accounts as compensation to them for their suffering in past.

An amount of Rs.20,000 per annum paid to 15 crores families totals Rs.3 lakh crores. There may not be more than 7.5 crores Dalit families in India, and an additional amount of Rs.75 lakh crores will suffice. Still the outgo of total direct cash transfers shall reach Rs.3.75 lakh crores, which is about 15 per cent of the total revenue of the government.

The caste system shall be eradicated. Only the former Dalits shall be paid 50 per cent higher amount than the other poor families in the country for a specified period agreed upon by all the political parties.

The Consumption of Tobacco, Alcohol, and Drugs: A Challenge for the Maha Mandir

The Islam religion bars its followers from the consumption of any form of alcohol; at the same time, the Sikh religion bars its followers from the consumption of tobacco in any form.

As things stand today in India, the consumption of alcohol has reached such a level that the women in poor families find it hard to survive. The husband loses his job because of extreme intake of countrymade alcohol and he insists that his wife provide him money to buy alcohol. Sometimes he also beats his wife and children in his quest for alcohol. The women in poor families are sometimes the breadwinners because their husbands are alcoholic. Many times, the women are forced into prostitution by their alcoholic husband.

The smoking of tobacco in the form of cigarettes and cigars has been a cause of major concern for more than a century throughout the world. Bidis and hookahs are the Indian form of tobacco smoking popular for centuries. It is amazing to learn that the Sikh religion, which is the last one to be added to the world religions, has barred its followers from any kind of intake of tobacco but does not restrict its followers from consuming alcohol. The entire world has only recently discovered that the consumption of tobacco causes cancer to the human body. By restricting the use of tobacco, the Sikh religion has definitely done a great service to its followers.

There is an increasing awareness throughout the world that the percentage of alcohol should be brought down in certain variants. There are lower taxes on drinks containing less amount of alcohol. It is heartening to see that the Islam religion does not permit its followers to consume alcoholic drinks.

The Hindu religion, in the absence of any apex authority, has been concentrating on less consumption of meat in any form. Still a good percentage of Hindus eat fish and other kinds of seafood. There are other Hindus who eat meat. Then there are Dalits, who have been consuming beef. There is no fixed identity for a Hindu that he should not consume non-vegetarian food or alcohol or tobacco or drugs.

The great Mahatma Gandhi was forced to take an oath by his local Hindu Vaishnava community before he left for London for his law studies that he will not consume alcohol as well as non-vegetarian food, which is the regular practice in Western societies. This incident is well known among all Hindus. Non-consumption of alcohol is not a Hindu belief; at the same time, more than half of Hindus also consume non-vegetarian food in one form or another, though there are certain Hindus who don't even consume onions and garlics.

The consumption of non-vegetarian food or alcohol is taboo in scores of Hindu families, but the consumption of tobacco is not. There is the tradition of chewing of paan among all Indian families, whether they are Hindus or Muslims. The chewing of tobacco was popularized by the habit of chewing paan a century ago among all Indians. The gutkha and paan masala are the recent phenomenon that happened after the independence of India. The people consume gutkha so they can chew tobacco without eating a paan. This kind of chewing of tobacco is not popular in other parts of world, and it has become a major cause of cancer in the Indian society. The government tries to create awareness about it but with little success.

Till now there has been no apex Hindu authority. The Maha Mandir can play a major role in educating and guiding all Hindus to keep away from the consumption of alcohol, tobacco, and drugs. The consumption of non-vegetarian food is not found to harm the human body, so the Maha Mandir need not discourage its consumption.

The Maha Mandir, in line with the Sikh community, can definitely ask all Hindus not to consume tobacco in any form. The sale of tobacco products need not be banned, but the Maha Mandir can definitely advice the entire Hindu community not to consume cigarettes and bidis or chew tobacco in any form, whether a paan or gutkha. This kind of move is going to help the Hindu community at large immensely, though it may not impose any penalties on anybody not complying with its advisory.

The old habits never die so easily. The Maha Mandir has to continuously instruct, guide, and educate all the Hindus not to consume tobacco in any form. The Maha Mandir has the example of the Sikh community by its side. The Swaminarayan sect of Hinduism also does not allow its followers to consume tobacco in any form. There is no reason why, over a period, the Maha Mandir will not succeed in its efforts. It can also force the Indian government not to allow any kind of advertisements promoting the consumption of tobacco in any form. At present the advertising of cigarettes is banned, but the paan masala are promoted by film artists. The government must stop such promotion. The Indian government has been lenient towards the consumption of bidis by the rural population and does not impose high taxes, which is the case with cigarettes. The Maha Mandir should see to it that the high taxes are imposed by the government on the consumption of bidis too. The harm done by the bidis is even more than the cigarettes to the human body.

The chewing of tobacco in the form of gutkha and paan masala has taken the young Indian population by storm during last three to four decades. People would chew the tobacco and also spit in public and create filth here and there. The Maha Mandir must educate all Hindus under its fold to stop the consumption of tobacco in any form.

Coming back to alcohol, the Gujarat State has banned the sale and consumption of alcohol since its inception in 1960. Though there is prohibition on alcohol, it is amply available to the people who want to consume it. So the prohibition on the sale and consumption of alcohol is not the answer to the problem. The Maha Mandir should impose a moral binding on all the Hindus that they should not consume alcohol in any form at any given time. India being a tropical country, the alcohol is not a necessity for the public. The country liquor available at nooks and corners throughout India at throwaway prices is the main culprit behind liquor consumption by the poor. The Maha Mandir must force the Indian government to see to it that the country liquor is neither made anywhere nor distributed. It will immensely help the women of poor families. In this regard, the Maha Mandir should have its own cell also to monitor the distribution of country liquor anywhere.

Only sometime back, the Supreme Court of India banned the sale of alcohol in areas near highways to discourage the truck drivers from consuming alcohol. But the decision had an adverse effect on tourism also, and liquor shops found their own ways to do their business. Entirely banning the sale of country liquor is the best way to discourage truck drivers from any intake of alcohol. The Maha Mandir should also see to it that the non-country liquor is taxed as per the content of alcohol in it. The higher the percentage of alcohol, the higher the tax. The liquor bottles should be available only at selected counters of high-end hotels and restaurants. The Maha Mandir can also propose to the government that the liquor should be sold only to the income tax payers at the presentation of proof of payment of income tax by individuals. This practice will prevent poor people from procuring alcohol from any source.

The consumption of drugs is a recent phenomenon. The main consumers are young boys and girls. Better policing can definitely curtail the use and spread of drugs. There are strict penalties on the possession of drugs by anybody throughout India, so there is no question on strengthening the laws on drugs. All that is needed is better policing.

A whole chapter in this book is devoted to weakly sermons or spiritual discourses by the apex head of the Maha Mandir. Mr. Modi, the prime minister of India, has been talking to the Indian population once a month in the *Mann Ki Baat* programme, but what a weekly discourse by the apex Hindu authority can do for all the Hindu population, the PM's *Man Ki Baat* cannot do. Many so-called babas, swamis, and god-men have been delivering lectures on morality to the Hindu population but without much impact. The existence of the Maha Mandir is surely going to impact the lives of all Hindus in a big way, and we can hope to curtail the consumption of tobacco, alcohol, and the drugs.

The Pollution of Rivers: A Challenge for the Maha Mandir

The cows are considered to be holy, and so have been the rivers for centuries by the Hindus. In old times, towns or villages took shape near a bank of a river or a lake or the seashore. It was necessary for the inhabitation of human populations that the water source should not be far away from where the people reside. Due to lack of development of medical science, the growth of the population was very low in those times and sometimes negative also.

The rivers, the prime source of soft water, were considered to be like mothers by all the Hindus. The industries did not exist in those times, and major sources of river pollution were the washing of clothes and the immersion of religious materials or ceremonial materials. The ashes of cremated dead bodies also constituted as part of pollution to river waters. In northern India particularly, people used to even immerse whole human corpses. into the rivers. The rivers like Ganga and Yamuna could absorb such human dead bodies because of their very huge flow of water originating from the Himalayas.

In modern times, things have changed drastically. India is home of a population of 1.3 billion human beings, almost hundred times than the population of 10–15 million a few centuries ago. The people in the old times never considered or thought that they would be polluting a source of soft water by washing clothes and immersing religious and ceremonial materials.

With a population of 1.3 billion in India, it is high time that the people treat the subject of pollution of river waters very seriously. For a number of decades, hundreds of crores have been wasted on cleaning the Ganga and the Yamuna but with very meagre results. It is due to the people's reluctance in complying with the necessity that they should not immerse the puja materials and the idols into river waters and that they must avoid washings clothes on the banks of rivers.

The pollution created by the industrial waste is a new phenomenon arising only about a century ago. The central governments as well as the state governments time and again try to enforce strict rules to stop water pollution but with little success. The industries have their associations to fight the government in a court of law to prevent any action. Corruption is another way to prevent the action on this front by the government officers. The result is that water pollution by the industries goes unabated.

The Maha Mandir can play a major role in stopping or in curtailing the pollution of rivers as well as all the water sources in India. Water pollution cannot be the subject of the Maha Mandir, but it can educate the industries and request the government machinery to take firm action against industrial polluters.

What Maha Mandir can definitely do is that it can educate all the Hindus not to pollute the waters by immersing idols or the puja materials in it. The government on its part has been trying to educate the people not to throw the puja materials into water sources, but the results are very slow. The immersion of idols in water is a major cause of concern for the Maha Mandir. In West Bengal, Durga idols of all sizes are immersed in water after the Durga Puja Festival. In Maharashtra and some adjoining states, the Ganesha idols are immersed in water after the completion of the Ganesha festival. A new, emerging trend is that Dasha Maa idols are now immersed in water after a ten-day festival in Rajasthan and Gujarat.

The Hindus need to learn from the example of Gujarat. Every year, the Navratri festival is celebrated in a big way as devotion to the goddess Durga during the same period of the Durga Puja festival in West Bengal. The people of Gujarat only keep a picture of the goddess Durga in the pandal and perform garbas in front it or around it. The Gujaratis don't immerse the photographs of the goddess Durga in water after the Navratri festival. There is no reason why the people of Maharashtra and West Bengal cannot follow the Gujarat culture of using photographs instead of idols of the goddess Durga or Ganesha.

The Maha Mandir is going to encounter resistance from the devotees of Durga in West Bengal as well as devotees of Ganesha in Maharashtra and the adjoining states. The people will cite the age-old traditions behind the immersion of idols in water. The Maha Mandir has to educate the people that the times have changed and that already inadequate water sources cannot be subjected to such pollution by the immersion of idols into them. The Maha Mandir can tell the people who still insist or advocate the old traditions that they should stop using electricity and modern gadgets if they want to follow the old traditions. The people have to change with the times, and the water sources are of utmost importance in modern times. The people cannot be allowed to pollute the waters in the name of old traditions.

It may take some time, but the Maha Mandir shall definitely succeed in convincing the people not to immerse the idols as well as the puja materials in water. At present, there is no apex Hindu authority in India, and a democratically elected government just can't dare to advice the people not to immerse the idols in waters. In some large cities, all the local government does is create separate ponds near the major water sources for the immersion of idols, but they meet with partial success only. Generally, the water sources of a city are large and spread over a huge area. People immerse the idols in water anywhere as per their convenience. Many devotees try to go deep into the water for the purpose of immersion and lose their life.

The government continuously talks about the cleaning of Ganga but hardly succeeds. Varanasi is known among all Hindus for the moksha if someone dies in that city. People bring the dead bodies of their near and dear ones from long distances to Varanasi for cremation on the banks of Ganga in the quest for a moksha for the deceased. Some people don't go for cremation of the dead body and simply throw it into the waters of Ganga. An elected government just can't do anything on this issue, but the Maha Mandir can.

The Maha Mandir, as the apex authority of Hinduism, can definitely instruct the Hindus to not pollute the Ganga waters any more. They can convince the people that times have changed. They can also seek the help of law enforcement agencies of the government. The politicians cannot do so in fear of losing votes.

The Kumbh Mela, Hinduism's greatest ritual, is held every twelve years at Sangam, Allahabad. Millions of Hindus take a bath in the holy waters of Ganga, Yamuna, and Saraswati (called Sangam at Allahabad).

This Kumbh Mela is a centuries-old tradition in Hinduism. Three subsequent Ardh Kumbh Melas are held at Haridwar in Uttaranchal, Nasik in Maharashtra, and Ujjain in Madhya Pradesh with a gap of three years between the two Kumbh Melas.

The Maha Mandir has to have a deep look at these Kumbh Melas, whether they should be allowed to continue in present form. The governments of Uttaranchal, Uttar Pradesh, Maharashtra, and Madhya Pradesh make elaborate arrangements for the success of all four Kumbh Melas, and the success rate is commendable. They have to arrange for the bath and stay of millions of people at the venue of Kumbh near the respective river. They take utmost care in providing fresh water for the pilgrims. All the arrangements by the government are at large admired by the pilgrims every time. During last Kumbh Mela at Allahabad, there was a small stampede, and a few people lost their lives. Perhaps it is inevitable when such a large gathering of millions of people takes place. The people took the stampede for granted.

There has never been an apex Hindu authority. No doubt, the Kumbh is a centuries-old Hindu tradition, but there is a huge difference in turnout of devotees in comparison to old times. The trains that provide connectivity to Kumbh sites only started in the twentieth century. Before that, only a few Hindus could attend Kumbh Melas. Along with connectivity by train, the population of India has raised manifold since the early part of the twentieth century, and the people also are more prosperous than they were about a century back.

The Maha Mandir must study the justification behind the state governments' efforts to promote the Kumbh Melas and attract more and more pilgrims to all four Kumbh sites. The Maha Mandir must study whether the water where the pilgrims take their holy dip is really clean or not and how much pollution is created in the waters of respective rivers by the bathing of millions of people.

The times have changed. The Maha Mandir cannot allow the devotees to pollute the river waters in the name of faith. A deep scrutiny of the devotees or pilgrims will reveal that almost three-fourths of them are very poor, poor, and poor middle class. These people are already living on limited economic resources. The Maha Mandir should take a relook whether these people should be encouraged to attend the Kumbh Melas, as they can make better use of their economic resources on education and healthcare for their children. The efforts by the state governments to attract more and more pilgrims to the Kumbhs burden railways in a big way, and the state transport systems are also badly affected. It becomes difficult for the common people who are not attending the melas to travel to their routine purposes. It may sound rude, but the Maha Mandir can consider recommending that the railways and the transport authorities increase their prices during the Kumbh Melas period. It will reduce the burden on them, and they will be able to carry out their task more efficiently.

The Maha Mandir should also stop free meals to the devotees if some charity organizations are doing so. The sadhus, *bavas*, and even beggars from all over India try to reach the site of Kumbh Melas during the period when they are held. The railway authorities are sometimes helpless and allow them to travel free of cost. The Hindu community considers the charity done at Kumbh Mela to the poor as a good deed; the rush of sadhus, bavas, and beggars is to collect the charities from these Hindu pilgrims. The Maha Mandir may consider appealing to the Hindu pilgrims not to do any charities at the site of Kumbh Melas. They can explain to them that this practice brings not only unnecessary rush to Kumbh but also brings antisocial elements. The

Hindus who can afford it have many other avenues for charity purposes. Hindus that cannot afford it need not do any charity and can spend the money on education and healthcare for their children.

A major attraction at the Kumbh Melas is the bathing of various groups of Naga bavas and other bavas. Now since there is a Maha Mandir in place as the apex authority of Hinduism, it is high time that the truth is made public about all the sadhus and bavas attending the Kumbh Melas and also spread it all over the country.

The Maha Mandir must go deep into the activities of all the sadhus and bavas. The public should know where these people in normal times stay and how they manage their livelihood. The people should also know how these people join such groups. The Maha Mandir must make sure that human trafficking is not involved in increasing the strength of sadhus and bavas. As mentioned in other chapters, the Maha Mandir must also scrutinize that the sadhus and bavas have no criminal background.

Coming back to the subject of water pollution due to religious practices of Hinduism, it is high time that the Maha Mandir educate and guide all the Hindus and at times issue advisories. The water resources are of utmost importance for the survival of human beings in present times, and the people cannot be allowed to pollute them in the name of religion.

The Pilgrimage Tourism: A Challenge for the Maha Mandir

As discussed earlier in another chapter, many followers of Hinduism take the worshipping of their god as fun and a matter of pleasure. The same is not the case with other religions. The fake gurus and god-men are found taking disadvantage of Hindus' mentality of seeking fun from the worshipping of their god.

Every year, hundreds of well-to-do or rich Indians travel to Haridwar and other places along with their relatives and friends. They arrange a religious ritual called Bhagwat Saptah, which is spread over seven days, and spend millions of rupees. The host looks ensures a comfortable stay for his guests as well as the performing team of Bhagwat Saptah. The main purpose behind the whole exercise is to increase the social influence of the host. This is a new phenomenon in Hindu society. Till now, the rich Hindus have been using marriages in their family to increase their influence over the society.

Certain Hindu temples have a tradition of flying a number of flags (*dhaja*) at the top of the roof of a temple. Many rich Hindus take pride in celebrating the hoisting of the flag on a certain temple in their name. They invite their relatives and friends to move along with them to the temple's location. They spend lavishly on this occasion. They arrange for a comfortable stay for their all the guests, along with good food. Once again it is a show of wealth in the name of religion.

The padayatra is a centuries-old tradition in Hinduism. In old times, there was no public transportation system, and people visited religious places by foot. They travelled distances in groups. In recent times, the padayatras have become organized to an extent that visiting the places of pilgrimage is more fun for the participants. The padayatra is organized by a certain travel agency for commercial gain or in the name of helping the poor to visit the places of pilgrimage. The people move by foot on highways in groups of twenties, fifties, and hundreds. Their meals on the way as well as their night stays are arranged by the padayatra organizers. This mania is picking up fast all over the country, particularly more in Gujarat, Maharashtra, and Madhya Pradesh.

The role of the Maha Mandir in case of such padayatras should be to enlighten the participating people as well as the organizers on the fact that in the modern world, the padayatras are not permitted on highways. It is the prime duty of any government to safeguard the interests of pedestrians as well as vehicle drivers. Therefore, it is imperative that the people of any faith or religion don't do any padayatra on state highways or national highways. There are only chances of fatal accidents in addition to slowing normal vehicle traffic. A fast and unhurdled traffic movement is a necessity in the modern times, and nobody can be allowed to obstruct it. Human lives are very important the world over, but in India, people do not value their lives accordingly. The government has not been restricting the padayatras on highways, though many people walking on highways are reportedly killed every day throughout India.

An elected government gives priority to the faith and religions of people and ignores their safety, but when an apex authority on Hinduism is in existence, there is no reason to ignore the people's safety as well as the rapid movement traffic on highways. As discussed in another chapter, the movement of Kavadiyas on highways during the monsoon period causes more problems than the normal padayatras, and many accidents occur every year. Sometimes, the Kavadiyas burn the vehicles and restrict regular traffic movement. The Maha Mandir must stop the Kavadiyas from their yatras.

Some devotees of Lord Krishna perform *prabhat pheris* early in the morning in urban areas. It is the right form of worshipping, as the followers chant songs without the use of loudspeakers. Such a practice needs to be promoted by the Maha Mandir, as it does not create any noise pollution; on the contrary, it is soothing to the ears of listeners.

In Hinduism, many kinds of rituals are performed by different groups or the castes on different occasions. At the end of a ritual or programme, the people perform a procession and travel through the city. In the old days, such processions were okay as life was slow, but in modern times, they cannot be allowed. The Maha Mandir must educate the people that they must avoid carrying out the procession on city roads.

People in India do take the worshiping of and devotion to a god as fun sometimes. The pilgrimage is not the only way of doing so. There are other ways also. With the passing of time, more and more people are getting economically better than before. The people participating in Hindu festivals have raised manifold after the independence. If 7 crores of people out of the total population of 35 crores in 1947 could participate in festivals. There are 70 crores of people now participating out of a population of 130 crores. Prosperity is a good thing to happen for the country, but responsibility comes along with the prosperity. That is what the Maha Mandir must convey to the people of India.

Things have gone to such an extent that there are dramas or magic shows in Ganesha pandals. The same is the case for Durga pandals in West Bengal. The garbas are performed in Gujarat during the Navratri festival every year. A new trend has picked up since the last two decades called disco garbas, which is more based on songs from movie for the fun of young boys and girls. Similarly, the Dahi Handi festival in Mumbai is now attracting thrills. Many participants are wounded every year, and some even die. The Maha Mandir must educate the Hindu devotees not to seek fun from the worshipping of a god, which is the case in all other religions.

Diwali and some other Hindu festivals are for the reunion of families; the joy of meeting other family members is associated with these festivals. The Maha Mandir should encourage such festivals but, at the same time, discourage the use of noisy firecrackers during the period of Diwali. Somebody's joy should not be the reason for the sorrow of others. Similarly, the Maha Mandir must discourage kite flying from the terraces and strictly ban the flying of Chinese tukkals.

To conclude, the common masses has a somewhat childish mentality, and the Maha Mandir must act in a parental manner, knowing what is good and what is bad in the interests of the common people.

The Poor Education System: A Challenge for the Maha Mandir

The readers must be aware about the fact that the Christian missionaries spread the message of Christ throughout the world, emphasizing on the education of the general masses. They did so centuries back.

Unfortunately, the Hindu caste system allowed only the Brahmans to teach in the Hindu society. The Brahmans in the old times felt insulted if they had to teach the Dalits, or the so-called untouchables, during those times, but it has no relation with the present state of poor education in India.

Before independence, the Britishers designed the Indian education system in a certain manner; it produced the clerical staff for the British officers in a huge manner. The industrial revolution had taken place in Europe and America by the time the Britishers penetrated India, but the Britishers were interested only in exporting to India the goods which they produced in England. So they went for an educational system which did not produce skilled workers in India. Still the quality of education in India was thoroughly disciplined.

After the independence of India from the British, various central governments as well as the state governments have been changing the education system frequently. The result is, only a percentage of students who graduate from Indian universities are employable. The same is the case for postgraduates as well as the engineers. In the early years after the independence, Prime Minister Nehru initiated the formation of IITs and many prime education institutions all over India. He called them the new temples of India, but the same cannot be said for the present state of educational institutes.

The successive governments at the centre have discouraged any profiteering from the education of the private entrants. The result is that politicians and large landholders without any experience have entered the field of education. Recently, a few well-reputed industrial houses have entered the field to impart quality education, but it is only like a drop in ocean.

Decades back, industrial training institutes were started throughout India to develop the skilled workers for the Indian industry. Initially, the results were good, but later on, the quality of education went down to an extent that hardly any ITI student was found employable by the industry.

The present government has taken a huge initiative in encouraging the Industrial Training Institutes in a big way, but the results are not encouraging because of the lack of good teachers.

Coming to the primary, secondary, and higher secondary education, a few years back, the then Indian government went for the Right to Education Act. The government made it mandatory for the private primary and secondary schools up to the eighth standard to accommodate students from poor families, using 25 per cent of their strength. The Indian government took pride in its efforts without acknowledging the fact that it is the duty of every government to impart free education to each and every student up to eighth standard, which is the practice throughout the world.

The difference between other countries and India is that it is only in India that the private schools are compelled to reserve 25 per cent of their seats for the poor masses. The fact is that the government is shirking its responsibilities of providing compulsory free education to its citizens. The government since India's independence has the necessary infrastructure in place for primary, secondary, and higher secondary education throughout India, but the people responsible for imparting education have destroyed the system over the last few decades in such a manner that the school buildings are in poor shape, the toilets are not usable, there are no instruments, and teachers are on payroll but absent. The midday-meal scheme is in place since decades ago to encourage village students to enrol in schools. The scheme has served its purpose to some extent, but it has taken a toll on education too. The teachers are supposed to be involved in preparing and serving the food every day. There are complaints about the quality of food also. Sometimes, in some schools, the students fall ill after eating the midday meal.

In the United States, the education imparted by the government schools is so good that sometimes even the well-to-do parents are in a dilemma whether to have their children enrolled in a private school or a government school. A couple of years back, the New Delhi government boasted about copying the US model, but the results so far are not so encouraging. Still there is no reason why the Indian government cannot impart quality education to all its students without burdening the private schools. Here the Maha Mandir has a ready role to play.

All over India, in almost all the cities with a population of above 2–3 lakhs, the Christian missionaries have been running higher secondary schools as well as some colleges also. They fall in the category of private schools, and the education imparted by them is of good quality. They teach with English as a medium as well as the vernacular language.

All the Maha Mandir has to do is take control of all the schools run by the Indian government. Since most of the money earned by the Maha Mandir is likely to be spent on cow protection, the Maha Mandir may not have any funds to spend on education. But the Maha Mandir can help to bring a sea change in the entire system. Presently, the Indian government finds itself helpless due to teachers' unions and has passed on a part of its burden to private schools.

There are over 110 million elders in the age group of sixty plus today. Almost one-third of them are residing in urban areas, and there are educated elders in rural areas too. The Maha Mandir can make good use of educated elders in managing the government schools in a better way. It will also benefit the elders in a big way as they will have a very constructive role to play in nation building and it will help them in passing time.

The efforts of Maha Mandir can yield almost twice the results than what the present government management does today with the expenditure of the same amount, though it is lower than the funds spent by other advancing countries in ratio of their GDP. The Maha Mandir has to see to it that the teachers are performing their tasks well and they are not absent. There are enough classrooms in every school. There should be separate staff to serve the midday meals to the students, and the quality of the food should also be good. There should be enough instruments in school labs. The toilets for both boys and girls should be in working condition and with running water. The schools' buildings as well as outer areas should be well maintained.

On top of it all, the knowledge and skills of teachers are of the utmost importance. The Maha Mandir has to set a mechanism whereby the teaching skill of each and every teacher is tested thoroughly so that the quality of education they impart to their students is proper. It may happen that most of the teachers will need to refresh their knowledge and skills. The Maha Mandir should force the teachers to spend extra hours to update their teaching skills. The same is going to be true in the case of students. Presently, in many cases, the knowledge of a seventh-standard student is only at par with a second-standard student.

It is going to be a huge task for the Maha Mandir to bring the learning of all the students at par with the standard of class they are studying in. The task is not going to be simple. In many cases, certain students may not be allowed to move to higher standards if they cannot attain the knowledge they are supposed to have. The teachers may devote few hours twice a week to update their knowledge and devote few hours on the rest of the days of the week to update the learning of students.

In the old times, the Hindu villages had only two holidays during a lunar month—one on amavasya and one on eleventh day of the brighter moon. It may seem cruel, but in present circumstances, sometimes both the teachers and the students should devote extra hours to correct the misshappenings in the Indian education system. Without doing so, the desired results cannot be achieved.

The Maha Mandir should have a separate cell to look after the education in all the government schools. It has to achieve what the government machinery cannot. The Maha Mandir shall have to be very strict in enforcing discipline in all the concerned players in the education system.

The sad thing is that the Maha Mandir shall have no funds of its own because of the cow protection crunch. It will have to depend fully on government funds. Still it can achieve almost 200 per cent results on the funds spent by the government in comparison to the results achieved by the present government machinery. The government will not be needed to burden the private schools by optimizing the use of present infrastructure available throughout India.

The Healthcare in India: A Challenge for the Maha Mandir

During the year 2017, it has been a matter of concern that hundreds of children died in hospitals due to one reason or another, including the lack of supply of oxygen. The healthcare is another area in addition to poor education in India where the Maha Mandir can play a positive role.

The readers may be aware of the fact that the Christian church played an important role in taking care of ill people as well as injured people in the early years of the industrial revolution, which included the development of modern medicine. During the Second World War also, the churches played an important role in treating wounded soldiers. Their dedications to both the education as well as the healthcare sector have helped the Christians in spreading their religion all over the world. There is no reason why the Maha Mandir also should not play an important role by simply helping the government in maintaining better standards of both the sectors.

India is a democratic country and the government has its limitations in the execution of their policies. The government cannot fire the teachers, doctors, nurses, or other staff from their jobs because of carelessness shown by them during their duties or by remaining absent. The Maha Mandir can definitely play as a buffer between the three—the government, the staff, and the service seekers (the students in the case of education and the patients in case of healthcare).

We already discussed the problems in the education sector, where the Maha Mandir can play an important role in improving the quality of education in India.

The problem with the healthcare sector in India is that the hospitals and the primary healthcare sectors are in poor shape. Recently, some state governments have taken action in improving the healthcare sector. They have improved the buildings and provided the necessary equipment also, but as the old habits die hard, sometimes the doctors are not available, the medicines are in short supply, or the equipment is not working because of lack of maintenance.

In the early days after the independence, India followed the socialist model of Russia. It gave a lot of empowerment to employee unions in all the sectors throughout India. The socialist system gave full security to the government's staff in their jobs without any commitment to their duties. The Indian economy has opened up to the global competition since 1990s, but the government's approach to its employees has remained socialistic as it was in the 1950s. This, along with corruption, is the root cause of the poor quality of the healthcare system in India.

Barring few states, the buildings of primary health centres and hospitals are in poor shape. The necessary equipment and instruments are in short supply as well as not well maintained. The medicines too are in short supply, or sometimes medicines used are old medicines with expired dates of use on them. Sometimes the doctors are on leave, or the hospital is short of doctors. The same is the case with nurses and other medical staff. Sometimes one doctor examines hundreds of patients in a day in a particular hospital or in primary health centre. Sometimes there is a dirty or filthy atmosphere all throughout the hospital.

Sixty per cent of India's population belongs to the poor class or lower middle income. Few of these people are covered by medical insurance, and they have to rely on the healthcare provided by the Indian government. Many times, these people who cannot afford it have to go to private a medical practitioner and pay from their own pockets for their treatment. India is a nation where more than 80 per cent of medical expenses are paid by the patients from their own pockets. The poor state of the healthcare system run by the government is responsible for that.

As discussed earlier in other chapters, extraordinary expenditure for cow protection of Rs.1 lakh crores per annum does not give the liberty to the Maha Mandir to spend on either the education sector or the health sector. All the Maha Mandir can do is to help the government in a proactive manner to run the machinery of the healthcare system in a better way so the patients can benefit.

Once again as mentioned in the chapter related to education, the Maha Mandir can take the help of retired elders in the age group of sixty plus. There are elders in India in excess of 11 crores, and at least 1 crores of elders are there to help the Maha Mandir in improving the state of healthcare throughout India. The Maha Mandir, while doing so, will be helping the elders also in passing their time in a constructive manner. A silver lining of Indian culture is that the people respect elders in their day-to-day life. Once an elder requests or directs a doctor or a nurse or a non-medical staff to do something, there are very little chances of a negative response. The elders can also play a very effective role in getting the cooperation of the public works department of a state in the maintenance of the building of a hospital or a healthcare centre. Presently, there is no coordination between the public works department and the health department of a state. The officers of a healthcare unit have their limitations in getting the necessary work done from other departments of governments.

Recently, during the last year or so, the Delhi State's government has earned a good name by running mohalla clinics throughout the city. Even *The Economist* has taken note of it. But the success is in its initial stage, and only time will tell whether the mohalla clinics are run effectively in future.

The Maha Mandir has at its disposal the knowledge of the healthcare system run by other countries throughout the world. The state governments also do have it but are not able to implement their knowledge effectively. The Maha Mandir is supposed to play a catalyst role in improving the quality of the healthcare system of India. It should not become a hurdle to the authorities of state health department.

The task of the Maha Mandir is not going to be any easy one. India is a vast country with tens of thousands of healthcare centres in rural areas. The first thing the Maha Mandir has to do is to teach all the healthcare sector staff empathy towards the patients. Till now it is apathy, which has resulted in the poor healthcare system throughout India.

On the government's part, it has to provide the necessary doctors, nurses, and other non-medical staff to fill the vacancies in all the government hospitals and primary healthcare centres. Without the necessary doctors and supporting staff, the healthcare system cannot be improved. The doctors, who have spent millions of rupees as well as pretty long years on their education, do not like to stay in villages. The government does have a bond with the medical students, compelling them to work in rural areas after the completion of their education. They have to pay an agreed amount if they don't fulfil the condition of the bond. Many of them pay the amount and don't go to villages. The government on its part must take the building of good roads as a priority between the cities and the villages. The doctors will not mind driving a distance of fifty kilometres every day by their own car from the city to the village, but a doctor will not like staying in a village.

In the present circumstances, some doctors do take up the jobs affiliated to hospitals in villages but are absent a number of times. The patients suffer. Sometimes only one doctor is present in a primary healthcare centre or a small hospital, and he has to examine each and every patient. The result is that the patients don't get the right treatment. The involvement of the Maha Mandir in monitoring the healthcare system is going to bring immense benefits to the healthcare seekers throughout India.

The Maha Mandir should create a separate cell to perform its task on the well-being of the Indian healthcare system. There are complaints from the authorities on healthcare centres that don't have enough doctors, enough supporting medical and non-medical staff, and stock of drugs and medicines. They also have complaints about the maintenance of civil amenities by the government authorities.

The Maha Mandir should not only work for the better facilities for the patients or service seekers; it should also look at the interests of the employees working at government healthcare centres. The Maha Mandir has to be very proactive. Neither the healthcare staff nor the patients should feel that an unnecessary hurdle is created for them in form of the Maha Mandir.

The efforts by the Maha Mandir are going to help the common man in a big way. In the course of time, we can expect the Indian healthcare system to deliver better results.

The Gold Holdings within Hindu Temples—Great Assets

*T*he Indians are known the world over for their love and passion for gold. The private holdings within Indian homes as well as within Hindu temples is supposed to be over 22,000 tons (worth Rs.65 lakh crores) in the year 2011, as per the gold council estimates.

The Indian government has only 550 tons of gold reserves with it against the 22,000 tons of gold held privately by the Indian public. Out of 22,000 tons of gold held by the public, 3,000–3,500 tons of gold (worth Rs.10 lakh crores) is lying within Hindu temples. This gold has been donated by the devotees to the various temples in the form of golden jewellery, bars, and coins. A few years ago, a treasure of gold worth an estimated $20 billion was discovered in secret subterranean vaults in the Shree Padmanabhaswamy Temple in Kerala.

The Indian government has come out with a gold depository scheme, and some temples have deposited some of their gold with the government.

When the Maha Mandir comes up, it needs funds for the construction of temples, buildings, and all the amenities of a small city spread over almost half a square kilometre, similar to the Vatican City State in Europe.

How are the funds going to be managed for the construction of Maha Mandir? The gold lying within Hindu temples is going to be a big boon for this purpose. After all, the Maha Mandir is for all the Hindus, and there is no reason why the Hindu temples should not unlock their treasures of gold with them for this purpose. It is going to be very unfair if the tons of gold lies unutilized and the funds are collected from the ordinary Hindus.

The management and the trustees of various temple trusts must know that the gold held by them belongs to the Hindu devotees. Till now there has been no apex authority as well as an apex priest in Hinduism. Once the Maha Mandir is in place as the supreme authority of Hinduism, all the Hindu temples will automatically be under its governance.

In response to the government's scheme for the deposit of gold, the trustees of some Hindu temples had certain reservations that the gold held by them belongs to the temple and the devotees and should not be melt. At that time, there was no talk of Maha Mandir or a supreme Hindu authority. Once the decision for the construction of the Maha Mandir is taken, it is going to be imperative for the convener committee to raise the funds for the construction after the land has been allotted by the government. The gold lying within the temples is quiet unproductive and should be utilized for some noble purpose. If the idea of an apex Hindu authority was not there, it could have been utilized for the creation of some educational institutions or hospitals.

All the Hindu devotees, if their opinions are taken, are certainly going to favour the use of gold lying within the temples for the construction of assets of the Maha Mandir. After all, the Maha Mandir is going to be for all the Hindus, and it may attract millions of tourists from overseas. We have the expertise of the devotees of the Swaminarayan sect for the construction of temples in the Maha Mandir campus. They have experience in building great temples out of India.

The convener committee shall be appointed once the government of India passes a bill in parliament for the creation of an apex authority of Hinduism. It will be up to the convener committee to look for the best options of fundraising. In my opinion, the best option is to utilize the gold lying within the leading Hindu temples.

After all, the Maha Mandir is going to be for the Hindus, managed by the Hindus.

Creation of Hindu Values: A Challenge for the Maha Mandir

*I*t's highly fascinating as well as surprising for many young Hindus to know that Hinduism is the oldest religion on earth, maybe about 5,000 years old, with followers of more than 1 billion people. It has survived till date without an apex governing body and an apex religious head.

The above fact has helped the Hindus to live in human society without a particular staunch character. There are scores of Hindus who eat non-vegetarian food. There are many who don't eat even onion or garlic. No Hindu is forced by a Hindu priest to visit the temples regularly. Some Hindus may not climb the stairs of the temple for years, and they are not questioned for doing so. Hindus are divided into a number of castes and subcastes. Hindus worship a number of gods and goddesses. Hindus speak many languages, and their festivals and traditions vary from place to place. Hindus have the most tolerant society on earth, and they respect other religions more than their counterparts. The end result of these kinds of diversities is that there are hardly any common Hindu values built over a period of time for the followers of Hindu dharma.

Now with the proposed creation of an apex Hindu body (with the suggested name of Maha Mandir), there is no reason why Hindu values are not created. The Christians are supposed to observe the Ten Commandments prescribed in the Holy Bible. The Hindus have no common religious holy text to follow, though some people take Gita as a guiding factor, but that does not offer an answer to Hindu values. Hindus are divided into four major varnas—Brahman, Kshatriya, Vaisya, and Shudra—in addition to Dalits, which is a separate division of Shudra for the purpose of sanitation and all related works.

Some country neighbours of India have been influenced by the Indian caste system. As a result, Buddhism and Islam followers in neighbouring countries have a section of people considered as untouchables. Even Japan, which follows Buddhism, has a particular section of untouchables, who carry out all sanitation jobs.

The purpose for the creation of the Maha Mandir is to eradicate the caste system from Hinduism. Once it is done, the followers of other religions in neighbouring countries will also see the back of untouchability. The caste system is not followed elsewhere in the world except India and its neighbouring countries.

Perhaps the division of Hinduism into hundreds of castes and subcastes has prevented it from attaining certain values. Once the caste system is abolished, there are fair chances that the values can be created by the apex authority governing all matters related to Hinduism.

Sticking to truth, no stealing, no adultery—these are some teachings common in all religions in the world and need not be taught to the Hindus. The Maha Mandir has to create some new values for all the Hindus which they can easily observe and adhere to. Non-consumption of tobacco can be one value the Maha Mandir can impose on all Hindu followers. Sikhism adheres to non-consumption of tobacco. Sikhism is the last addition to all the world religions, and if the Sikhs can avoid the consumption of tobacco, there is no reason why all Hindus cannot do so.

'Smoking cigarettes is injurious to health' is widely promoted by all the governments throughout the world, but no particular religion other than Sikhism has prohibited the consumption of tobacco. Rural India consumes bidis more than cigarettes every year, and the Indian government considers bidis as an indigenous product and does not discourage its use at par with cigarettes.

The smoking of tobacco is a common thing all over the world, but the Indians chew tobacco in different forms, which has picked up with the passing of time, reaching alarming levels. The Indian government does educate the people not to consume chewable tobacco, and the results are not encouraging. The Maha Mandir can play a major role in convincing all Hindus to stay away from all the forms of tobacco. Still it does not need to prohibit Hindus from the consumption of tobacco in any form; otherwise, it will only lead to more corruption in Hindu society.

To create certain values in Hindu society, the chief priest of Maha Mandir should have dialogues every week with fellow Hindus. Many American presidents do so, and our Prime Minister Shri Narendra Modi also does so once a month in his *Mann Ki Baat* broadcast. The Christian churches have a sermon every Sunday, but with the availability of the electronic media, the chief Hindu priest can make the best use of radio and TV as well as the mobile to deliver his Hindu sermons.

The chief Hindu priest can definitely educate all the Hindus on the non-consumption of tobacco more than the Indian government. Another way for the Maha Mandir is to come out with clear guidelines that no Hindu shall consume tobacco in any form. It may also insist that it's a sin to consume tobacco. In the long run, the sermons by the chief Hindu priest are definitely going to serve this purpose.

The consumption of alcohol in the form of country liquor by the poor and the underprivileged Hindus is another major problem. Islam prohibits its followers from consuming alcohol. The Gujarat State in India also has a prohibition policy, but it has not succeeded to an extent that other Indian states can follow its model. The country liquor is amply available throughout India, including the state of Gujarat. The poor people who become addicted to such liquor lose their job, and they beat their wives in their quest for money to buy liquor. In some cases, certain poor addicts force their wives into prostitution to extract money for liquor.

The Maha Mandir can definitely play a catalyst role in preventing country liquor consumption in India. It can force the government to see that the country liquor is not produced anywhere in the country. It is a very well-known fact throughout India that the producers of country liquor are working with the local police department. The Maha Mandir can create a special cell to monitor the availability of country liquor.

The chief Hindu priest can educate all the poor Hindus to stay away from any form of alcohol and use the saved money on education and healthcare for their children. Like in the case of tobacco, the Maha Mandir can issue clear guidelines to Hindus not to consume alcohol if they are not income tax payers. It does not mean that the Maha Mandir should encourage the income tax payers to consume alcohol, but there is no other way if full prohibition on alcohol consumption is not imposed on all the Hindus. The Maha Mandir should also work with the government in a proactive manner to see that more and more liquors with lower alcohol content are available.

The standard-quality liquor should be available only in posh areas and should be sold to the income tax payers only. The liquor with lower alcoholic content should be taxed less. In the long run, efforts by the Maha Mandir shall definitely have an impact on the consumption of alcohol in the country.

Regarding drugs, the Maha Mandir can take a clear stand that no Hindu shall consume drugs in any form. All over the world, drugs are generally prohibited, but only recently some mild forms are permitted. The Maha Mandir should leave it to the government to form a policy on drugs, but morally, it can educate all Hindus not to go for drugs.

The prostitution is the oldest profession in the world, and it did exist in India too before thousands of years. The Maha Mandir should educate all Hindus to stay away from it but, at the same time, should consider getting the profession of prostitution legalized in favour of the unlucky females who have been forced into it due to poverty or human trafficking.

The Maha Mandir can play a very effective role in curbing human trafficking in India. It can have a special cell to monitor such a practice.

Gambling is not official in India, though such a vice is limited among Hindus. The character of Yudhisthira is famous among Hindus for gambling and losing even his wife while doing so. The betting on sports activities, particularly cricket, is the new form of gambling, which did not exist in the times of Yudhisthira. Many advanced countries have legalized betting on sports to prevent the underground activities related to it. The Maha Mandir can clearly guide all Hindus to stay away from any kind of gambling as well as betting on sports, but at the same time, it must seriously consider if it can insist that the government legalize betting.

The Maha Mandir can also insist and educate all Hindus about fake babas and all sorts of superstitions. Particularly in rural areas, even today many people seek the superstitious way instead of proper medical treatment. The Maha Mandir must educate all Hindus to go for the right scientific ways in all the aspects of life. There is great confusion among all Hindus about the Mahabharata and Ramayana, whether they are part of history or only great epics. The Maha Mandir must clarify its stand on this matter. The faith about these two epics is so deep among Hindus that even educated people feel shy in accepting that they are not part of history. Some Hindus even take pride in citing examples in the Mahabharata and Ramayana that show that science in India in those times was much more developed than the modern times. Recently, even in some science congresses, some Indian scientists have such a view. The Maha Mandir must see to it that people do not believe such myths.

There are so many programmes about mythology now appearing on TV. The Maha Mandir must educate the viewers that the mythology is not part of history at all.

Hinduism suffers from too much intake of mythology in day-to-day life. Once the Maha Mandir is in place as the apex Hindu authority, it will discourage the rise of fake babas throughout the country. It should be the endeavour of the Maha Mandir to educate all Hindu devotees to assess everything scientifically and not accept a thing blindly in the name of faith. Shani Devta is the latest addition in mythological beliefs. Many temples have emerged in so many towns, and many TV programmes have also come up.

The Maha Mandir has a major task of teaching the art of consensus to all Hindus. It is a centuries-old weakness among all Hindus that it is tough for them to reach a consensus on any subject. It became a popular quote during the 1960s that the Indian brain is equal to two Japanese brains but five Japanese are equal to a hundred Indians. It shows lack of teamwork among Indians.

The Indians are divided by caste, creed, languages, religions, colours, eating habits, and geographical areas. People from one caste try to accommodate the candidates of their caste into the government jobs. Similarly, people from one particular state may try to accommodate candidates from their state. The game goes on endlessly, and the whole country suffers. It is high time that Indians learn the art of consensus.

The history of economically successful countries reveal that they have succeeded because they could reach a certain consensus on related subjects and move on. Unless and until Indians improve themselves in this aspect, progress is going to be slow, and productivity also is going to remain low. The Maha Mandir can definitely play a major in eliminating this major flaw from the character of Indians. They have to learn teamwork. The task is not an easy one, but only the Maha Mandir can do so.

An old weakness in Indians is that they pass judgement on others without proper knowledge. The youngsters in families are taught in Hindu culture to respect their elders, but the elders are not supposed to be proactive with the youngsters. This is not the case in other societies. The Hindus must learn to respect other individuals irrespective of whether he is older or younger. This kind of mindset is a must in modern times.

In the old times, elderly Indians could treat the females and the children as their properties. The mindset in urban areas among economically well-to-do Indians has changed a lot but lots of Indians suffer from the old mindset. There are so many cases of sexual violence against women because of old mindset among men. Any amount of strict penalties for such conducts are not going to succeed unless the mindset of such Indians is changed. The Maha Mandir can educate the Indian men every week to respect each and every woman. The process will take years of persuasion by the Maha Mandir but will definitely yield results in the long run.

The same is the case in how children are being treated by their parents belonging to the poor, very poor, and lower middle class. It is more due to low education and economic backwardness. Things will improve when these families attain better education and economic prosperity, but the Maha Mandir cannot wait for it. It must go on educating such families to change parents' actions towards their children. They must treat their children with respect, which is the case in all modern societies.

In the old times, the people with some shortcomings, whether in physically or because of the lack of blessings by the god, have been hated by people, and it was permitted by the culture. A widow was not supposed to be present on a happy occasion in a family. Similarly, the appearance of a handicapped person—maybe with the loss of one eye, hand, leg, or some other part—was treated as a bad omen by the Hindu society. Such people were not supposed to be present when religious rituals were going on. Things have changed, but not entirely, leaving a scope for the Maha Mandir to educate on this subject.

The respect for elderly parents has been the core belief in Hinduism. Due to the shrinking size of families, some people are now finding their aged parents as liabilities. This new phenomenon is attributed by the Indians to the Western culture, which is not the case. In Western society, the elders reach old-age homes by their choice. They are not forced by their family members, which is the case in Indian society. The Maha Mandir can play a very positive role in educating the Indians on this subject.

The Jyotish Shastra and Vastu Shastra are branches of Hinduism. The Maha Mandir should treat the practitioners of Jyotish Shastra as well as Vastu Shastra as service providers and the Hindus as service seekers. It must educate both of them, particularly the service seekers, to act with utmost caution. Perhaps the Maha Mandir can ask the government to restrict the appearance of advertisements by the Jyotishis and Vastu Shastris in print media as well as electronic media.

It should be the endeavour of the Maha Mandir to pursue and educate all Hindus to study the scientific aspect of every issue and then believe in it. It should have a special cell to monitor that no dubious people are taking advantage of the lack of scientific knowledge of the people.

One unnecessary problem prevailing in Hindu society is child marriage. In the old times, even before the independence, the boys got married even before the age of eighteen and girls before the age of fourteen, sometime before the age of puberty.

It's heartening to see that the Indian government in the earlier years of Indian democracy framed the rules prohibiting child marriages and fixed the age of eighteen years for the female and twenty-one years for the male for eligibility for marriage. The government did not put forward the argument about population control; it only argued that neither boys nor girls are ready financially or educationally to bear the burden of having a child at such an age. Millions of Indians, particularly in rural areas, did not comply with the rule and went for child marriages. Had they observed the rules, the Indian population might have been lesser today by at least 3 to 5 per cent.

Only recently, the honourable Supreme Court of India had to intervene with a decision that if a girl below eighteen is married and she complains, her husband can be legally penalized for any sexual relations with his wife.

Till now there has been no Maha Mandir. The situation is ripe for it to take a clear stand on child marriages. The Maha Mandir should educate and guide all Hindus not to go for child marriages as it is not in the national interest. If any such marriage takes place, the people concerned must be arrested and penalized as per the law.

The concept of Khap Panchayats, or some panchayats in other forms in rural areas, has been prevalent particularly in northern India for centuries in delivering quick justice in relation to all local problems in rural societies. The Britishers did not intervene and allowed them to operate.

In a democratic country, such panchayats for the delivery of justice cannot be tolerated. The Maha Mandir must give clear guidelines to all Hindus to scrap all such panchayats.

Over a period after the independence of India, the Indians have developed an image of being law-breaking citizens rather than law-abiding citizens. The Maha Mandir has a task before it on this front. The habit is formed among the Indian citizen because of irrational laws framed by the Indian government after the independence.

The Maha Mandir, before educating the citizens, should educate the Indian government to form rational laws and keep the taxes lowered so the Indian citizens can stop being lawbreakers. Once the laws are rational, the citizens must abide by them.

The Formation of the Maha Mandir

It is a well-known fact as well as a matter of pride for many Hindus that Hinduism has survived for thousands of years without an apex governing body and apex priest.

There is no doubt that Hinduism can survive for thousands of years more without an apex governing body, but the need has risen due to the mess created by caste-based reservation in India, encouraged by politicians. Seventy years have passed by after India attained independence from British; there are no signs of any abatement of the problem. The politicians or the policy makers can't be relied on, so there is a need for the formation of an apex body to govern all issues related to Hinduism. Another reason is that in the absence of an apex governing body of Hinduism, the present Indian government is championing the cause of Hinduism, resulting sometimes in chaos in the case of cow protection due to overenthusiasm of the so-called cow protectors.

The proposed apex governing body of Hinduism, once in place, shall not only be able to eradicate the caste system from Hinduism; it will also be able to handle cow protection, thoroughly helping the Indian government to devote its valuable efforts on governance rather than on some petty matters related to the Hindu religion. The greatest hindrance in the formation of an apex governing body is going to be the Hindu mindset of not reaching easily a consensus on any subject.

After the due debates in the print media as well as electronic media, the government has to decide that it wants to go for the formation of an apex Hindu authority. Then the government has to bring a bill in the parliament and get it through with the approval of the members of both houses. Once the bill is passed, the government has to form an ad hoc committee for the formation of the apex Hindu body along with a prominent religious person to head it.

Once ad hoc committee is formed, the government has to look for suitable land for the project. A piece of land measuring about five hundred acres or so in Uttar Pradesh and near the capital city of Delhi is going to be the best bet. After all, proposed the Hindu Vatican is going to attract millions of tourists every year, and it will be better if it is easily accessible by road, rail, and air. Another choice could be the 600 acres lying vacant in Haryana that had been vacated by the convicted Dera Guru Ram Rahim. If the government finds it suitable for the purpose, it can issue an ordinance to acquire the land then hand it over to the ad hoc committee. A few years back, there was an incident in relation to a large plot of land near Mathura which was vacated by order of a court. That plot can also serve the purpose.

After acquiring the necessary land for the construction site comes the issue of finances. As discussed in an earlier chapter, all the Hindu temples are going to be governed by the proposed apex Hindu authority. It is estimated that the combined holdings of gold by the temples is in excess of 3,000 tons with a value of about Rs.10 lakh crores.

The construction of all buildings as well as the creation of all facilities related to the apex Hindu authority—or we may call it the Maha Mandir—is not supposed to cost more than Rs.1 lakh crores. The Indian government can issue an ordinance forcing all the temples to part with 10 per cent of their gold reserves for the formation of the Maha Mandir so funds will not be a problem. Many temples may claim that they are autonomous bodies and may not comply with the ordinance of the government. It is up to the government to prevail over them.

Then comes the construction of various temples reflecting the different faiths of Hinduism. The Swaminarayan sect, which is famous for the Akshardham temple in Delhi, possesses the expertise to create of high-quality temples throughout world. They can be entrusted the task of constructing all the temples as well as related amenities. There is no reason why the authorities of Swaminarayan sect should not oblige.

Thus, the land, the money, and the expertise to build the temples related to the proposed apex Hindu authority, Maha Mandir, are not going to pose any problem. All the Indian government has to do first is to decide on it and then get a bill passed in parliament. Simultaneously, the government can appoint a convener along with an ad hoc committee under him to frame the constitution of the apex Hindu body. The government can give the committee a certain time period, maybe three months or six months.

During the period when the committee does its work on framing the constitution, the government can arrange for the land and pursue the temples to spare the necessary funds in the form of gold. The construction related to the Maha Mandir can begin only after it.

Once the constitution related to the Maha Mandir is ready, its head can be elected along with the governing body. The apex Hindu body can start functioning from any place offered by the government or any Hindu organization and need not wait for related buildings and construction to be completed. If an ashram or any other institution at present is large enough to accommodate the functioning of Maha Mandir's activities, a separate city or premises may not be created. It may save both money and time.

Conclusion

I have lived for more than sixty years in Gujarat, the land of Mahatma Gandhi. I have observed the casteism prevailing in high degree, more so in part of western Gujarat, called Saurashtra and Kutch. I have observed people asking for the caste of a trader or service provider before buying goods from him or seeking his services. I have come across customers responding with joy, 'Oh, you are from Baniya community, then no problem.'

One very positive thing I have found in Gujarat is that people from the so-called higher castes treat even Dalits with respect. Perhaps it is so because of the impact of Mahatma Gandhi's ideals. I also observed the economically well-to-do people in Gujarat treating the poor people with respect. It's very heartening. Why it can't be so throughout the country, barring the casteism part of it?

I have been a strong advocate of eradicating the evil of casteism from Hinduism. The ongoing cow protection movement has encouraged me to pen this book since now these are two major issues related to Hinduism.

On the front of the eradication of casteism from Hinduism, I have tried to learn about the views from cross sections of society. Most of the people agree to the idea but express great reservation that it cannot be achieved in the present circumstances. I don't agree with them, and there is no reason why the idea cannot be given a try.

On the front of cow protection, I find the people getting surprised to learn about the exorbitant cost of Rs.1 lack crores required annually for cow protection. There is no doubt that the cow is a holy animal for all the Hindus.

The apex body of Hinduism is now the need of the hour. If such a body is not formed, how long will the Indian caste system go on? Perhaps it will go on endlessly as the Indian politicians cannot be expected to work in the direction of eradicating the caste system. No political party would like to commit hara-kari, or political suicide, by committing to the public that it will work towards the abolition of the caste system.

In the absence of an apex body of Hinduism, the ruling Bharatiya Janata Party at the centre and in many states has taken up the Hindu cause of cow protection. Since India is a secular country, it will be just if all Hinduism-related matters are taken up by its apex body when it is in place.

I have proposed the name Maha Mandir for the apex Hindu body. Once it is in place, it is going to help immensely the Bharatiya Janata Party. It can definitely take the credit for the formation of the Maha Mandir while it is in power. There is no doubt that the BJP and the RSS are the true champions of the Hindu cause, but the formation of the Maha Mandir is going to help them in devoting all their time to governance rather than indulging in petty matters related to cow protection.

Abolishing casteism is the issue which is going to benefit the country as well as all the political parties in the long run. Once the newly formed Maha Mandir eradicates the caste system from Hinduism, no political party will be held responsible for disfavouring the Dalit community and other backward communities. The pride and self-esteem of Dalits as human beings is going to be restored in the long run. The idea of depositing 50 per cent more amount under the direct fund transfer scheme in the accounts of Dalits may satisfy them and pave the way for the total eradication of the caste system from Hinduism.

Some people may argue that the Dalits will continue to be addressed as Dalits if they are paid more. It is not so. Dalit families are supposed to be paid more as compensation for the inhumane treatment tolerated by them for centuries from the so-called upper-caste Hindus. Once put in action, the higher amount shall go to all the Dalits, irrespective of their economic strata because it's compensation.

The Maha Mandir, once formed, is going to be useful to all Hindus in many ways. The tourists from other countries visiting India shall have another attraction in the form of the Maha Mandir. People don't forget to visit the Vatican when they visit Italy or Rome.

The Maha Mandir is also going to help in the creation of values in the lives of Hindus. The head priest of Hinduism is going to be regarded by all, and his teachings are going to be taken seriously. The Maha Mandir can work wonderfully well in changing the mindset of Indians on women's safety. Any amount of new laws are not going to work in that direction, but sermons from the apex Hindu authority can definitely work. The politicians or the celebrities from any field cannot be expected to carry out such a task. India is very much short of icons today.

The Maha Mandir is also going to be very useful in educating Hindus to Stay away from all self-proclaimed fake babas and god-men. Similarly, it is going to be very useful in educating Hindus on non-consumption of tobacco, drugs, and alcohol. It is also going to be very useful in keeping Hindus away from all sorts of superstition activities.

I hope the readers will find the idea of the Maha Mandir applicable.

The Hindu Vatican

*H*induism has survived for thousands of years without an apex governing body as well as an apex priest.

The author, Suresh Agarwal, explores the possibility of the formation of an apex body to govern all matters related to Hinduism. In his opinion, it is the only way to eradicate the caste system prevailing in Hinduism. The apex body, once in place, shall be able to perform many tasks on Hinduism, including cow protection.

The subject of creating a Vatican sort of place in Hinduism is contemporary and very germane to the prevailing circumstances in India.

www.ingramcontent.com/pod-product-compliance
Lightning Source LLC
Chambersburg PA
CBHW062204280526
45788CB00001B/443